OVER
LAKELAND
FELLS

30 Walks across the Magnificent Foothills

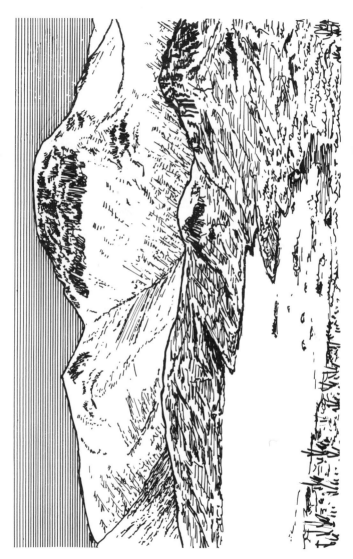

Midwinter on Haystacks: the Gables from Innominate Tarn

OVER LAKELAND FELLS

30 Walks across the Magnificent Foothills

by

Paul Hannon

HILLSIDE   PUBLICATIONS

HILLSIDE PUBLICATIONS
11 Nessfield Grove
Exley Head
Keighley
West Yorkshire
BD22 6NU

ISBN 1 870141 10 5

Printed in Great Britain by
Carnmor Print and Design
95/97 London Road
Preston
Lancashire
PR1 4BA

CONTENTS

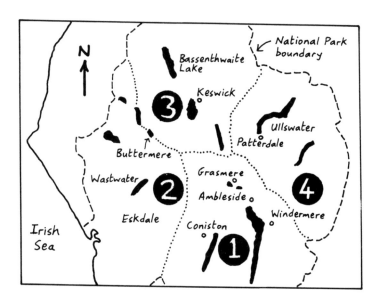

INTRODUCTION

What sets Lakeland apart from so many upland areas is the profusion of delectable lower tops. These fells often stand in the shadow of our greatest mountains, yet retain their individuality, appeal, and special character to offer a less strenuous challenge with not dissimilar rewards. Favourites such as Catbells and Silver How share equal billing with a range of less glamorous fells, all with much - not least of all solitude - to offer.

Inevitably these lower- but definitely not lesser - heights appeal to a greater range of walkers than the more demanding peaks, from parents introducing their inquisitive offspring to the delights of the hills, to ageing fellwalkers slowly losing their battle with the giants. Indeed, many an active mountain walker would do well to turn his attention occasionally to these less elevated gems: in addition to their other merits, they regularly provide new and unexpected angles for viewing the surrounding peaks.

Although most fells are linked in some way to continuing higher ground, virtually all the walks in this book are devised to avoid the feeling of having only climbed half-way: each walk gains at least one individual summit that is sufficiently detached to instil that magical feeling of being 'on the top'. Indeed, quite a number of the walks remain entirely aloof from the high mountains, with the likes of Lord's Seat and Black Combe being very much the masters of their respective groups.

The lower fells regularly throw up their share of accident statistics, for their tantalising accessibility can often draw from his car the ill-equipped visitor who would never consider a climb onto the lofty heights above. Substantial crags and poor weather are not the preserve of the high mountains, and the precautions that they demand should be applied equally to the fells in this book. Most basic requirements are solid footwear, adequate clothing and waterproofs, and some form of food should the walk unexpectedly prolong itself. The ability to use map and compass cannot be over-stressed.

Although the purpose of the guide is to supply all necessary details of the routes, the accompanying maps serve only to portray them, with the role of supporting the relevant Ordnance Survey map. Although the information at the start of each walk gives details of both 1:50,000 and 1:25,000 sheets, the latter (in most cases the Outdoor Leisure Map) is a far more useful companion on the hills. The guide is divided into chapters dealing with four well-defined areas, which between them offer a walk in most corners of the district. The average length is a modest 5½ miles, sufficient to occupy a leisurely half-day but short enough to either extend or move onto something else later in the day.

KEY TO THE INDIVIDUAL WALK MAPS

▲ main summit

△ other top

ridge

the route

alternative or relevant path

road

lake or tarn

beck or river

woodland on or near route

major crags

● ▪ village/farm

+ church

TABLE OF FELLS ASCENDED

Fell	Metres	Feet	WalkNo
Black Combe	600	1968	9
Haystacks	597	1958	12
Middle Fell	582	1909	10
Ard Crags	581	1906	16
Hartsop above How	580+	1903+	28
Outerside	568	1863	15
Angletarn Pikes	567	1860	26
Knott Rigg	556	1824	16
Lord's Seat	552	1811	22
Hard Knott	549	1801	8
Calf Crag	530+	1738+	4
Caw	529	1735	7
Crag Fell	523	1715	11
Mellbreak	512	1679	13
Beda Fell	509	1670	30
Wansfell	487	1597	1
Gowbarrow Fell	481	1578	25
Lingmoor Fell	469	1538	3
Barf	468	1535	22
Barrow	455	1492	15
Catbells	451	1479	17
Binsey	447	1466	24
Stile End	447	1466	15
Arnison Crag	433	1420	27
Steel Knotts	432	1417	29
Low Fell	423	1388	14
Gibson Knott	420+	1378+	4
Fellbarrow	416	1365	14
Grange Fell	410+	1345+	19
Helm Crag	405	1328	4
Silver How	395	1296	5
Hallin Fell	388	1273	29
Walla Crag	379	1243	20
Latrigg	368	1207	21
Sale Fell	359	1178	23
Loughrigg Fell	335	1099	2
Holme Fell	317	1040	6
Castle Crag	290	951	18

Chapter One

SOUTHERN LAKELAND

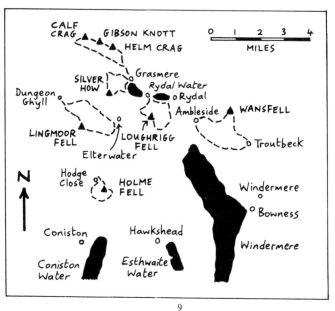

WALK 1   WANSFELL   1597ft/487m

> *Start: Ambleside*
> *Map: 1:25000 - SE; 1:50000 - 90*
> *8 miles / 1700 feet / 3¹₂-5 hours*
> *Parking: Several car parks*

Leave the Market Place by the road running behind the Salutation
Hotel, signposted 'To the waterfalls.' When adjacent Stock Ghyll parts
company on the left, do likewise by taking the path shadowing it into
the adjacent woodland of Stockghyll Park. Within minutes the cata-
racts of Stock Ghyll Force are in full views, the path climbing to their
right. On gaining parity with the falls, turn right on a level path that
doubles back to leave the wood at a redundant antiquated turnstile.
Emerging opposite the college, turn left on a rough drive until just
beyond a cattle-grid, where a stile on the right marks the commencement of the ascent proper. A path climbs a field to the terminus of a
green lane, then continues up more steeply with extensive retrospective views unfolding over Ambleside to the Langdale Pikes and part
of the Fairfield Horseshoe. Towards the top occasional rock outcrops
add interest and soon the cairn on Wansfell Pike is gained, across the
fence that spans the top. With less than a quarter of the walk
completed, all the work is done!

Although this is not the true summit of the fell, it is as far as most
people venture, and in fairness, the main top along the ridge offers
little over and above this. While the unadventurous can therefore
head straight for Troutbeck on the well blazed path continuing the
line of the climb, the rest of us will turn left with the thinner path
along the broad ridge. Almost at once a wall replaces the fence, and a
very pleasant walk ensues. Beyond an intervening rise the wall
trends left of the true watershed, and a slender path remains true to
the height of land. Soon the summit is gained, marked by a cairn, with
another wall just below.

Across the wall is an eminence that on modern maps appears to

Caudale Moor and Thornthwaite Crag
from Wansfell

raise itself to a height equal to the long established summit, though there can only be the odd centimetre in it. The descent from the cairned summit commences by doubling sharply back to the right, the sketchiest of paths being admirably served by a series of cleverly sited cairns on prominent alps. These lead down to a wall, exactly at the point where it converts into a green lane. This is the head of Nanny Lane, which can be followed down without further ado into the scattered village of Troutbeck. This walled byway is an absolute charmer, being green and lush for most of the way - during which time it absorbs the direct descent path from the Pike - forming a curious natural stone layered surface further down, and culminating as a veritable rutted watercourse that can only do a sound job in dissuading motorised transport from gaining and ruining the delectable upper sections.

Turning right along the road, a goodly portion of Troutbeck is experienced (note the several wells on the right) before reaching the Institute and Post Office with its faded wooden signs on the wall corner. A little further on the road is the 17th century statesman's house at Townend, just short of which a walled path can be used to climb back up to the main route, which is the rough lane branching up to the right from the Institute. This is Robin Lane, a grand byway that climbs only gently as it swings round Wansfell's southern flanks. A little beyond a pillar up to the right, the lane is vacated at a profusely signed gate on the left, from where a good path takes up the journey. This time height is lost as it drops down to a bridge where a surfaced drive climbs up to High Skelghyll Farm, in view for some time.

From a gate at the top end of the farmyard a wide track runs along to enter Skelghyll Wood, and soon a sign indicates the branch path to Jenkin Crag, just yards to the left. Returning from this renowned viewpoint the broad path continues down through the trees, swinging right to bridge lively Stencher Beck then soon right again to run a level course out of the trees, with views now over Waterhead to the Coniston and Langdale fells. Merging into a drive and then a lane, the way descends onto Old Lake Road as it is about to join the main road through Ambleside. Turn right along this quieter back road for a long walk back into the centre.

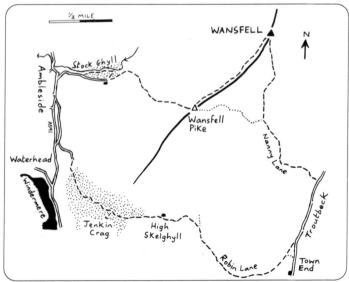

WALK 2   LOUGHRIGG FELL   1099ft/335m

> *Start: Rydal Water   GR 350065*
> *Map: 1:25000 - SE; 1:50000 - 90*
> *4 miles / 1000 feet / 2-3 hours*
> *Parking: Large car park below the*
> *main road at the head of the lake*

Before starting the walk it should be noted that of all the popular ones in the book, this one in particular draws the crowds, if only to the environs of the lakes and the lower slopes.

From the car park take the broad path heading upstream with the Rothay. A short way beyond the toilet block the river can be crossed by a high footbridge (note the wetlands conservation area immediately downstream) to take the path heading directly away into the trees. It rises steadily to leave the wood, and here turn right up to a seat on a knoll. Grasmere is now laid out below, and with a choice of paths opt for that rising steadily to the left. This is Loughrigg Terrace, a time-honoured favourite that slants gently across Loughrigg's flank with Grasmere's beautiful vale seen at its very best in the fullness of autumn. At the end of the terrace, do not go into the trees but turn up to the left to commence the climb proper. An initially steep path scales the fellside, evidence of its popularity being all too obvious in the necessarily restored sections. When the going eases a rise is topped and the summit appears just across a small depression.

The top is marked by an Ordnance column between small upthrusts of rock, and is one of the few felltops to be regularly gained by your average motorist. Much of the surrounding valley scenery is obscured by Loughrigg's own sprawling flanks, but to the west the ground falls away sufficiently to reveal a glorious prospect of the Langdale valley, from shimmering Elterwater up to the dalehead protected by Bowfell and the inimitable Langdale Pikes. To resume the walk leave the crowds behind by continuing south - in the direction of Windermere - on a clear path. This drops to a trough between undulating knolls, becoming a broad green swathe that follows the

The summit of Loughrigg, looking north to Seat Sandal, Dollywaggon Pike, Great Rigg and Fairfield

general line of the ridge, such as it is. When a wall briefly comes in on the right, divert up to a prominent cairned top ahead for a sudden surprise view of Loughrigg Tarn.

The path continues meanwhile, but drops down to the left before the final knoll where a smaller cairns sits high above Ivy Crag. If incorporating this section, return to the main path to continue as crags abound hereabouts: Loughrigg may be a wonderful playground but it is not without its dangers. As the path drops down, a wide, marshy depression is seen below, and it is here that a good portion of Loughrigg's extensive path network converge. Cross to its far side and take a green path heading left, rising steadily to a brow on the skyline ahead. Keeping all of the marshy tracts well to the left, the brow is topped and the path begins a descent back towards Rydal Water.

An inviting minor top on the right may demand a detour, while across to the left, the folds and tors of Loughrigg's higher slopes suggest a far greater altitude for this fell. As height is lost the rough wall of Nab Scar across the valley increases its dominance, and is soon seen in better proportion as Rydal Water, tranquil as ever, at last appears at its foot, along with the white painted Nab Cottage.

Eventually the path comes down to meet a broader one at a bridge, and turning left it rises immediately to one of Loughrigg's enormous caves, mute memorials of quarrying days.

Just beyond it a larger yawning hole is more easily accessible and invites a paddle into its darker recesses. Yards beyond it the path forks at one of Loughrigg's numerous seats. Either can be taken, though the level upper one is probably best. When it forks bear right, and on nearing the lower path bear right again to reach the gate into the woods just ahead. The initial steps of the walk can now be retraced back to the start.

If keen to continue, the walk can be prolonged by keeping straight on at the second fork to reach the seat above the gate into the woods, and this time taking the downhill path to the prominent upper bridge just below the outflow from Grasmere. Downstream paths on either bank will then lead back to the first footbridge.

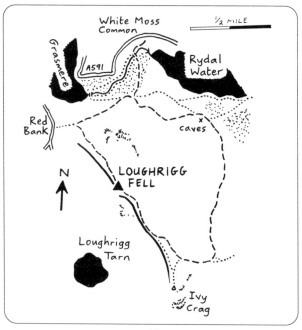

WALK 3   LINGMOOR FELL   1538ft/469m

Start: Dungeon Ghyll Old Hotel   GR 286060
Map: 1:25000 - SW; 1:50,000 - 90
8 miles / 1600 feet / 3¹⁄2 -5 hours
Parking: Large car park alongside hotel

From the car park return to the main road then turn right and sharp left. At the first bend a stile and footpath sign point the way into the campsite on the left. At the first opportunity turn off the drive into the trees on the right, where a footpath rises to cross a field and up through more trees to a stile onto the fell. A steep climb with stunning retrospective views of the Langdale Pikes then ensues in the company of a wall, easing out to arrive at the summit of the Blea Tarn road connecting the two Langdale valleys. Without joining the road go up behind a memorial seat to a gap in the wall, from where a path sets off on a contouring course parallel with the road below. At a fence it joins another path to climb up to the saddle at the foot of imposing Side Pike.

Turning away from it, a pleasant green path heads up to the right alongside the wall. After a short climb the wall is crossed at a stile above a corner, and the path continues up the other side, taking a series of stony outcrops in its stride. The going soon eases up and a beckoning false summit is reached: this is the last spectacular view-point for the Langdale Pikes. The main top is now only a few minutes further, crowned by a cairn that well confirms its superiority.

On leaving the top almost three-quarters of the walk remains, commencing by crossing the adjacent stile and heading away with the fence. Little height is lost as the ridge of the fell continues south-eastwards, a thin path remaining with or close to the wall that takes over. After a slight rise to a slate cairn on the right, the bracken level is reached and the path immediately becomes very distinct. Various evidences of defunct slate quarrying activity are passed, though the most impressive, an alarming, gaping cliff face on the very ridge top, will be missed unless a brief detour is made to peer - with extreme

16

The Langdale Pikes from Lingmoor Fell

caution - down it.

From here on, a multitude of green pathways weave down through the bracken, and it matters little which is taken. At a wide green crossroads the right arm gives an opportunity to detour out to a prominent cairn above Bield Crag, a classic Little Langdale viewpoint. With the wall as ever close at hand, the main path steepens to zig-zag stylishly down by a small beck to a stile in the bottom corner. Swinging round to the left the path meets a further stile before joining the unsurfaced Elterwater-Little Langdale road above Dale End Farm.

Turn left along it until it enters a wood, then branch left on a wide path. This rises slightly to a miniature pass in the trees before heading off tidily between crumbling walls, and dropping down to cross a track to arrive at an isolated dwelling. Rather surprisingly a surfaced road is joined, and this is followed to the left for a long woodland walk to Baysbrown Farm. A rough surfaced road takes up the journey beyond the farm but this is forsaken as it bends steeply up to the left, in favour of a wide path heading on through the trees. On drawing level with the next set of buildings, at Oak Howe, turn sharp right to approach them, then left in front of the barn to continue updale on a delightful walled green way.

At the premature demise of the enclosed track, the path forges on along the base of Lingmoor Fell (look for the pinnacle of Oak Howe Needle high above), with Great Langdale Beck in its deep channelled course below. Past a sheepfold in a wall corner the path strikes down across the fields to Side House, but then carries on behind it to a stile in the wall ahead. The final section carries on in the same vein before petering out above the campsite, entered through a marshy tract and a stile. Head on through to the far end to retrace steps along the road back to the car park.

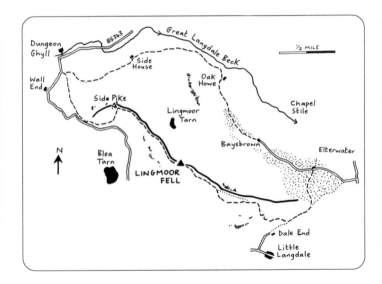

WALK 4 HELM CRAG
GIBSON KNOTT
CALF CRAG

1328ft/405m
1378+ft/420+m
1738+ft/530+m

> *Start: Grasmere*
> *Maps: 1:25000 - SW or SE (either omits a tiny section only)*
> *1:50000 - 90*
> *8 miles / 2000 feet / 3¹/2-5¹/2 hours*
> *Parking: Large car parks in the village, and a very small one*
> *on Easedale Road (actually on the walk) which saves a little*
> *distance but is soon full*

Leave the green in the village centre by Easedale Road, which sets off from the bookshop corner in the direction of the youth hostels. Keeping doggedly on, it enters green pastures while surprisingly maintaining its solid surface, losing it only at the small collection of desirable properties across the field. When the continuing rough track turns sharply left above the houses, a fork is reached and the climbing can commence. The path to the right sets off on a winding course that follows a heavily restored line up Helm Crag's flank, avoiding the first few hundred feed of the old path that is being left to recover from erosion. Just before it is rejoined on the ridge-end, with its anticipated view down into the Vale of Grasmere, a pause to look ahead up the valley of Far Easedale will reveal the whole route, including the two other tops to be visited. Once on the ridge-end only a short but lively clamber up through the outcrops remains before the summit ridge is gained.

There can be no other felltop quite like Helm Crag, for this is a bewildering wonderland that demands careful exploration. The highest point will be found at the far end of the short ridge, where a tilted tower of rock points skyward. Known by various names, best as the Howitzer, what is certain is that an adventurous scramble is required to claim to have gained the fell's true summit. Helm Crag is better known to many tourists as the Lion and the Lamb, and it is usually

Helm Crag summit, with Steel Fell behind

the grouping of rocks first encountered that give rise to this title.

Next top along this main ridge dividing Far Easedale and Greenburn is Gibson Knott, and the way thereto is straightforward. A cairn just beyond the rock tower signals the start of a short but rough descent, from where a much gentler pull leads onto Gibson Knott. The main path in fact cheats on the ridge proper, and outflanks several outcrops by traversing the Far Easedale flank below the skyline. Two cairns adorn the top, the lower being rather a better viewpoint for Easedale.

The path continues unfailingly westward towards Calf Crag, but again exhibits a preference for the Far Easedale side of the ridge and avoids one or two more sporting opportunities. After gentle ambling it climbs a little past Pike of Carrs, a prominent feature from the valley, then encounters an unappealing marshy plateau before the final section to the summit. Thankfully this is a grand spot to struggle to, for the neat cairn sits amidst outcrops above a steep fall to the valley. This is also the place for which to save the sandwiches, far from the throngs venturing only as far as the Lion and the Lamb.

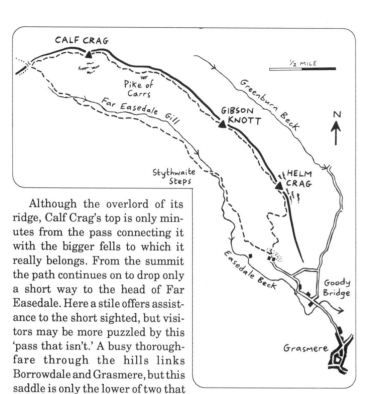

Although the overlord of its ridge, Calf Crag's top is only minutes from the pass connecting it with the bigger fells to which it really belongs. From the summit the path continues on to drop only a short way to the head of Far Easedale. Here a stile offers assistance to the short sighted, but visitors may be more puzzled by this 'pass that isn't.' A busy thoroughfare through the hills links Borrowdale and Grasmere, but this saddle is only the lower of two that the route uses, the main one being the pass of Greenup Edge beyond the head of Wythburn.

Whatever its status it is good enough for us, so turn left to commence an infallible return to Grasmere. The path soon crosses to the south bank of Far Easedale Gill above some falls, until well down the valley where it returns to the other side. Here, Stythwaite Steps have been rendered redundant by a less inspiring footbridge. Below this the path broadens into a stony track to return to the houses of Easedale, to then retrace steps back to the village.

WALK 5　　　SILVER HOW　　　1296ft/395m

> *Start: Grasmere*
> *Map: 1:25000 - SE; 1:50000 - 90*
> *3¹⁄₂ miles / 1100 feet / 2-3 hours*
> *Parking: Car parks in village*

Leave the green in the village centre by the lane leaving a crossroads by the cafe next to the Heaton Cooper gallery, and within a couple of minutes it transforms into a parkland drive. Ignoring the left fork to Allan Bank (one of Wordsworth's former homes), continue uphill to its demise at an enviably sited farm. From the gate to its left an enclosed path climbs to emerge onto the open fell. An undemanding if steep pull then leads up through a rich cover of juniper.

Shortly before escaping out of these rampant little trees watch for a left fork, indicated by two small but strategic cairns: far more useful and aesthetic than the monstrous piles scattered about the fellsides. The path leads across to Wray Gill, which is followed upstream a short way before crossing the temporarily tamer little ravine in colourful surroundings. On the gentler slopes opposite a few sketchy yards precede the path's clear return, and at a substantial cairn the summit appears ahead. Only the final climb brings any steepness to this upper half of the ascent.

On leaving the summit cairn head south, a sketchy path materialising to aim for a prominent cairn a quarter-mile distant. Once at the cairn continue a little farther to drop down to a level path. Turning left here, a corner is rounded to arrive at a sprawling cairn at another path junction. The path heading left is the return route, although a brief foray to the right will bring an improved and final view into Great Langdale, the ground falling away dramatically above the environs of Chapel Stile.

The return to Grasmere calls for little description, the path being clear throughout and giving ample opportunity to appraise Grasmere's lake in its green vale. The descent is everywhere well graded, the path ultimately becoming enclosed to debouch onto the Red Bank road opposite the boat landings. All that remains is a short walk to the left back into the village.

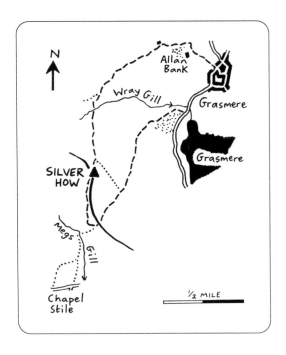

WALK 6　　　　HOLME FELL　　　1040ft/317m

> *Start: Hodge Close　GR 315015*
> *Map:　1:25000 - SE or SW*
> *1:50000 - 90 (and a tiny part on 96)*
> *4 miles / 600 feet / 2-3 hours*
> *Parking: On old quarry land on the roadside*
> *between Holme Ground and Hodge Close*

From the ruin at the southern end of the southernmost of two monstrous quarry holes, go through the gate and take the stony path up to the right to a second gate. Past the small spoil heaps just ahead, leave the wallside track by a track slanting back up to the left. At the former quarry site take the central path rising straight up to a reservoir that once served the quarries but now does an admirable job serving nature. Already the summit is plainly in view, ahead and to the right of the prominent Ivy Crag. A path runs along the right bank then bears off to the left to rise to the prominent dip on the skyline that is Uskdale Gap.

Up to the right of this impressively named saddle, a path climbs towards the summit. An obvious detour can be and usually is made to the large cairn on Ivy Crag, from where the highest point of the fell beckons across a minor col. The elongated summit ridge is usually gained by a weakness in the craggy rim defending its eastern side, and the highest cairn stands to the southern end on a tilted slab. The fine panorama extends from the great bulk of Wetherlam immediately adjacent, to the beautifully wooded low country around Tarn Hows. Of particular note is the full length view of Coniston Water stretching away.

To commence the descent return to Uskdale Gap, and turn down the path to the right. Soon entering a wood, it drops down pleasurably to meet a level path at a large cairn. Turning right along it, this waymarked route (white arrows) runs along to arrive at a stile and gate just above Yew Tree Farm and the Ambleside-Coniston road. Without descending the broad track to the farm, turn right above the fence, a track materialising to undulate along beneath the craggy southern buttresses that belie this fell's modest stature. This permissive path, still waymarked, becomes a wonderful green track through lovely surroundings to emerge onto the Hodge Close road at Shepherd's Bridge.

Turn right for more than half a mile before a bridleway sign is reached on the right. From it another smashing track rises steadily with a wall, mostly through woodland but also across an open pasture above Holme Ground Farm on the road below. Beyond a gate a path branches right should one wish to climb Holme Fell again, but otherwise keep on for a couple more minutes to rejoin the outward route just short of the start.

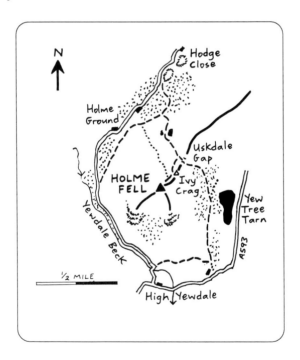

Chapter Two

WESTERN LAKELAND

The Scafells from Middle Fell

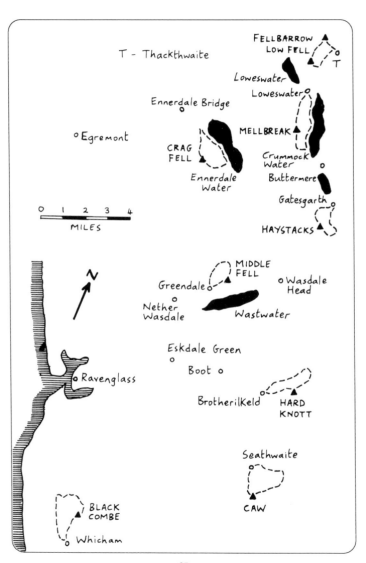

T – Thackthwaite

FELLBARROW
LOW FELL
T

Loweswater

Loweswater

Ennerdale Bridge

MELLBREAK

○ Egremont

CRAG
FELL

Crummock
Water

Buttermere

Ennerdale
Water

Gatesgarth

HAYSTACKS

```
0  1  2  3  4
MILES
```

MIDDLE
FELL

Greendale ○

○ Wasdale
Head

Nether
Wasdale

Wastwater

Eskdale Green
○

Boot ○

○ Ravenglass

Brotherilkeld ○

HARD
KNOTT

Seathwaite

BLACK
COMBE

CAW

Whicham

27

> *Start: Seathwaite   GR 228960*
> *Maps: 1:25000 - SW; 1:50000 - 96*
> *6 miles / 1600 feet / 3-4 hours*
> *Parking: Rather limited. There is a small*
> *lay-by just past the church, and several*
> *other spaces further north, all handily*
> *placed on the return route*

From the church head back towards the Newfield Inn, but at the sharp
bend just before it take a gate on the left. A stony track known as Park
Head Road rises unconvincingly between walls, but through a second
gate it turns right with the wall and the route is then obvious.
Remaining stony for a while, it rises gently with the wall through trees
and on up the fellside. A few hundred yards beyond an intervening
gate, a wide green track doubles back sharply to the left. It is the
access road to the former Caw Quarry, and maintains the undemanding nature of the ascent. This splendidly engineered track expires at
the slate workings after a short zig-zag up to a ruined hut and a dark,
dripping level. The summit is still several hundred feet up the flank
behind, but a thin path, partly cairned, bears half-right up the slope.
As height is gained it becomes less clear, by which stage it is as easy
to strike back up to the left to conclude in style, the Ordnance column
appearing well before it is gained.

    The column is cemented into a rock ridge that forms the summit,
which makes a splendid place to be, aside from its outstanding merits
as a viewpoint. On a clear day pride of place goes to the Scafell line-
up around the head of Eskdale, though the length of the Duddon valley
is rarely seen in such detail. To the north-east the bulk of the nearby
Coniston massif keeps a watchful eye behind the craggy wall of White
Pike, its nearest top. This is also the direction to take, heading down
to the minor depression across which the rocky little top of Pikes is
more than prominent. Keeping left of rough ground just below the top,
the saddle is soon reached and a five minute pull leads onto Pikes'

Looking back to Caw from Pikes

cheerful little top.

From Pikes a similar line calls for another drop to a marshy depression, where a green track will be found running along its far side. On the western flank of aggressive-looking White Pike the former Walna Scar Quarries are now prominent, and the track makes for them after rising imperceptibly left to escape the marshy ground. An upright slate marks the minor brow, from where the track undergoes a transformation and contours along to the spoil heaps as a delightful green way. Beyond the various remains the track continues above a wall, and at a gateway a path turns down to slant across to the Walna Scar track, short-cutting the normal route which continues on past an isolated spoil heap to meet the broad track at its own gate.

Either way, turn down the track for an uncomplicated and speedy return to the valley. Near the dale floor it becomes surfaced as the Water Board road from Seathwaite Tarn joins in, and keeping left at a minor junction the road meets the valley road above Seathwaite Bridge. Bearing left again this quiet road is now followed back down

to Seathwaite, in the delightful company not of the Duddon itself, but
the effervescent Tarn Beck.

Harter Fell and the Scafells from Walna Scar Quarries

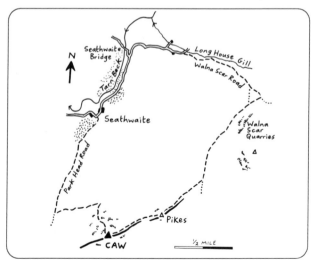

WALK 8   HARD KNOTT   1801ft/549m

> *Start: Brotherilkeld, Eskdale   GR 211011*
> *Maps: 1:25000 - SW; 1:50000 - 89 or 90*
> *5 miles / 1600 feet / 2¹⁄2-4 hours*
> *Parking: Roadside parking area at foot of*
> *Hardknott Pass, just above the cattle-grid*
> *above Brotherilkeld*

This walk is something of a break from the majority in this book, in that most of the time spent on the fell is away from regularly used paths. Settled weather is required not only to aid navigation but also to appreciate the mountain panorama. A useful pointer is to only commence the walk if the higher tops are free from cloud, as in any case it would be almost criminal to miss out on their contribution.

From the cattle-grid head up the pass, and when the left-hand wall breaks away, leave the verges of the road in favour of a green path rising up to the left to gain the exciting remains of the Roman fort of Hardknott Castle. Like a castle in the air it guards Eskdale, astride the line of the Roman road between *Galava* (Ambleside) and *Glannoventa* (Ravenglass). After a potter round, head for the north-west gateway overlooking the upper section of Eskdale. A path runs along the outside, so turn right along it above a pronounced drop to the valley. At once there are stupendous views across the deep trough of the Esk to the mighty peaks of the Scafell range, and along with the pyramid of Bowfell to their right, this wild bunch will continue to dominate the scene.

Though never more than sketchy, the course of the path is fairly self-evident, rising gently along the grassy shelf above the fall to the left: high up to the right, the rock-defended cone of Hard Knott's subsidiary, Border End, repels any attempts at climbing in that direction. Continuing to rise above the wall of Yew Crags ahead, the slim path crosses the remains of a wall above it and heads on, virtually level and fading all the time, to the head of a splendid ravine between tall rock walls, a grand moment. Rounding a corner just beyond, all signs of the trod have gone, and ahead slopes of scree tumble to the Esk.

While the river seems a long way below, the freshly revealed chain of crags up to the right seem more distant still. At this point the tower of Eskdale Needle can be discerned by the keen eye, being set in the crags left of centre but not yet appearing detached from them. The aim now is to scale the grassy flank between minor outcrops up to the amphitheatre below the crags. The sooner more height is gained the sooner the Needle will present itself, and indeed when it does, one will wonder how it escaped attention for so long. With surprising ease one should soon be virtually level with it, and can then simply contour across to the beckoning pinnacle.

Having explored its environs double back and turn up through another old wall just above. Only yards further a conspicuous grass gully on the right will lead quickly up to the top of the fell. A marshy plateau can be avoided by going left alongside a line of rocks, after which a rock barrier precedes the final defence, another fringe of rock with the cairn perched on a boulder defiantly above. Aside from the obvious features of the view, a good section of the Duddon valley from Wrynose downwards reveals itself.

Descent is a prolonged affair, beginning by turning north along the broad and in parts marshy ridge, with the long south ridge of Esk Pike, between the Scafells and Bowfell, offering itself as a guide. Our ridge is novel in that it declines in towards the mountains, and thus further enhances the vista across to the high fells. Beyond a steeper grassy drop a negligible rise leads to a small cairn on a knoll. Beyond this all is grass, and across to the right the neck linking Hard Knott with its parent fell Crinkle Crags above the head of Mosedale is visible, while to the left Cam Spout falls into Great Moss in the lap of the Scafells. Before waiting for the very end of the ridge it is as easy to incline slightly left to drop to the distinct path tracing Lingcove Beck.

Turning down to the left a steeper drop soon ensues above the exuberant waters of the beck, to descend to the graceful arch of Lingcove Bridge. Here Lingcove Beck joins the Esk, and in this delectable corner one could easily while away an hour or two. Without actually crossing the bridge our path continues downstream, and within yards the newly charged Esk breaks into tumbling falls and crystal pools: this is truly a walk in heaven. Up to the left meanwhile the dark tower of Eskdale Needle breaks the skyline, watching over the tremendous plunge of fellside from Hard Knott's cliffs.

Beyond a stile the path crosses two rough grazing enclosures to regain the riverbank, which is then accompanied tightly downstream to Brotherilkeld Farm. The farm road bears right to run out onto the main road, just below the cattle-grid at the foot of the pass.

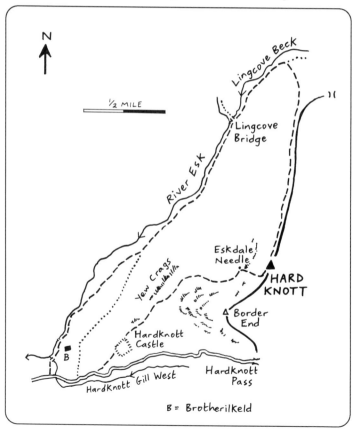

WALK 9   BLACK COMBE   1968ft/600m

Start: Whicham Church   GR 135826
Map: 1:25000 - Pathfinder 625 (SD08/18)
1:50000 - 96
5 or 10 miles / 1900-2000 feet / 2¹∕₂-6¹∕₂ hours
Parking: Parking area at the church, up a short
drive (not the adjacent farm road) off the
A595 a half mile north-east of Silecroft

Pass through the short snicket between the church and the former school, and turn left along the lane to Kirkbank. As a rougher lane it continues behind the house to debouch onto the open fell. Turn immediately right up to a gate and stile, from where a wide green track commences a steady climb above Moorgill Beck. This same broad pathway is as infallible as could be, and leads to within yards of the summit. Out of the head of the gill the gradients ease, the distinct second half of this ascent being on a slanting course across the extensive upper reaches of the fell. A novel and refreshing feature at this stage is that the views are largely of a vast expanse of water, such is this fell's unique proximity to the coast. At a sharp bend just before the top - where grass returns for the final feet - the path forks: the left one skirts the top, the right one climbs steeply up to it.

The highest ground is a sizeable plateau, in the centre of which an Ordnance column is ringed by a large, crumbling stone shelter. On Black Combe the view is of paramount importance, to the extent that it would almost be sacrilege to make the climb in poor conditions. Only if falling upon appalling conditions, however, should one fail to cross the plateau eastwards, for here the barren top falls away in the dramatic tangle of crag and scree known as Blackcombe Screes. Whatever one's route of return, this enormous amphitheatre must be inspected in order to appreciate Black Combe as more than a grassy mound.

Two alternative routes of return are given, though by far the most popular will be the simple retracing of steps, highly recommended

White Combe and the Duddon Estuary
from Black combe screes

thanks to the nature of the path, the seaward views, and the bullseye of hitting the starting point. The alternatives are as follows:

1) return to the bridleway west of the summit, and pick up its initially less clear course continuing northward. As it descends the north-west shoulder of the fell (aiming for Bootle and Ravenglass) it improves, always making a gentle job of dropping towards the coastal plain. On reaching a fence turn left along the bridleway, which drops down to the ruin of Hall Foss then runs for a considerable time above the intake wall. This course along the base of the mountain is clear throughout and for the most part excellent underfoot, to eventually arrive at a former mill complete with crumbling water-wheel in situ. In this lovely corner an enclosed access track is joined, and followed along and eventually down to the main road at Whitbeck.

Turning left along the verge for some 400 yards, a footpath sign points the way to 'Black Combe'! Not that this is our objective, but it is intended to indicate a path running parallel with and only yards above the road. Depending on usage it may prove arduous, but an improved link to it further on (opposite Wood House, the first buildings on the road) rises and continues up to a gate in the fence above. Without going through it, turn along to the right on a better path that soon splits, the second branch to the left probably being best. It surmounts the minor brow, and, still below the fence, runs along above a wall to a lone house. Its drive is then followed away, and within a minute or two proves to be the rough lane whereby the fell was gained at the outset.

2) This alternative continues north atop the full length of Blackcombe Screes and the less substantial Whitecombe Screes, then bears right at a saddle to connect with a green drove road descending gracefully into the enclave of Whitecombe Beck. It crosses the beck and continues down to the intake wall, where the right of way runs on through Whicham Mill to the main road. As this leaves a two-miles road walk, the usual variation is to remain above the intake wall, where a green path through the bracken runs all the way back to cross Moorgill Beck to where the walk gained the fell above Kirkbank.

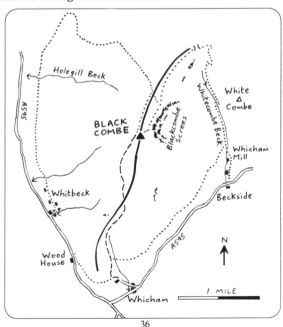

WALK 10   MIDDLE FELL   1909ft/582m

Start: Greendale, Wastwater   GR 144056
Map: 1:25000 - SW; 1:50000 - 89
4 miles / 1650 feet / 2-3 hours
Parking: Verges before the road becomes enclosed
at Greendale Farm, the first buildings on the
Gosforth road branching off the lakeshore road

By the side of the buildings an inviting green path heads for the fell, soon climbing more steeply through bracken. At this early stage the cliffs of Buckbarrow up to the left dominate the scene, until that is, one looks back to see the inimitable Screes already looking majestic across Wastwater. At a distinct corner above Greendale Gill the path forks. That turning into the gill will be the return route, but for now take the green track scaling the foot of the broad ridge up to the right. It is soon guided by small cairns through a rash of boulders, but then fades to a narrow trod. Keeping more to the stonier ground of the ill-defined ridge on the right, the vague path re-establishes itself, though remains slender throughout the rest of the climb. In clear conditions - the only ones to be on Middle Fell - the use of the path is immaterial on this pleasant climb. On the summit the path runs a few yards west of the cairn, but this substantial, colourful edifice will take some missing.

The view is occupied entirely by the magnificent Wasdale scene, where every member of this famous cast seems keen to get in on the act. Across the sombre waters of the lake far below, Illgill Head sends down the great fans of the Screes, while to the left the famous grouping of the Scafells overtop all else. Moving around, the unmistakable cone of Great Gable rules the dalehead, and Kirk Fell peeps over the lower but far more interesting-looking Yewbarrow. Further left still, the less acclaimed heights of Red Pike, Scoat Fell and Haycock make their own worthwhile contribution.

To resume the walk return to the path and follow its course northwards, declining gradually towards the broad saddle with the bulk of loftier Seatallan. As the thin path fades at the col, turn down to the left for Greendale Tarn. The marshy terrain above the tarn should be given a wide berth by keeping high above its right (west) bank. On nearing the tarn foot it is then safer to turn down to it, where one can accompany either bank of the cheerful stream away. That on the opposite side is clearer, once it appears, while that on the near bank keeps out of the restrictive confines of the gill to offer wider views over to Whin Rigg at the foot of Wastwater. On approaching the twin ravines of Tongues Gills, the grassy tongue of Brown How deflects the thin west bank path down to the beck, to cross Greendale Gill and thus join the other path. The left-hand of these ravines sports a splendid series of vertical falls, well seen from the path. Continuing downstream the path returns in grand style to the outward junction to retrace steps back to the road.

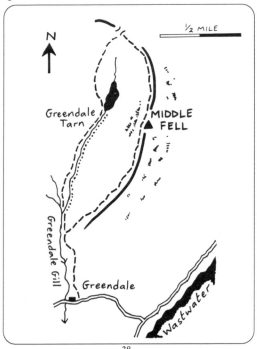

WALK 11   CRAG FELL   1715ft/523m

Start: Ennerdale Water (foot of lake)   GR 085153
        Maps: 1:25000 - NW; 1:50000 - 89
        5 miles / 1400 feet / 2¹⁄2-3¹⁄2 hours
Parking: Forestry Commission car park at Bleach
        Green Cottages. This is reached by taking the
        Croasdale road out of Ennerdale Bridge, then
        turning right in half a mile to the road end at
        the bridge over the lake's outflow.

From the car park cross the bridge over the Ehen and bear right up
past the cottages, on the drive to prominent Crag Farm at the base of
the fell. It actually stands at the foot of Grike, close relative of Crag
Fell which itself begins at the conspicuous ravine of Ben Gill, directly
ahead. Before reaching the environs of the farm a wide track branches
off to the right, retaining the farm's privacy to cross to a gate in the
wall ahead. Here turn right on a track along the base of the plantation,
until before reaching trees on the right a track doubles back up to the
left. In existence before the trees were planted, this initially roughish
way improves into a splendid grassy path, not merely preserved but
actually flourishing as it slants up to leave the plantation behind at
a stile.

Slanting even more gently now it runs along to approach the head
of Ben Gill's ravine. Where we cross it is but an unassuming stream,
but there are splendid views down it, backed by the lakefoot. Beyond
this delectable spot for a sojourn the path begins to climb again, soon
above a well defined grassy scarp that proves to be an extension of the
wall of Revelin Crag. The path keeps well above the cliffs and when
the going eases up, the summit cairn is just a short level stroll.

In deteriorating conditions one would be well advised to retrace
the outward route back to the lakefoot, but in favourable weather the
first thing to do is step nearer the northern edge to obtain the more

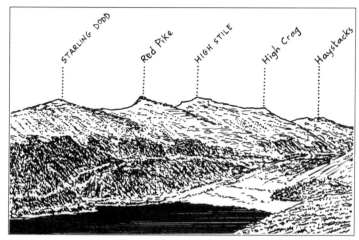

Across Ennerdale Water from Crag Fell

dramatic views over Ennerdale Water. To commence the return turn south-east down the grassy flank, aiming towards the saddle with neighbouring but distant Iron Crag, occupied by the upper limits of a plantation on Crag Fell's featureless southern flank. The views up the valley to a rim of famous peaks are truly memorable, and if not crossing all the way to the forest fence, a potter round the modest remains of iron mines can be included.

In either case, keeping left of the forest fence a very solid wall climbing the fellside will be neared. Deflecting down to the left a wall junction is soon reached. That scaling the fell is in excellent repair and obviously intended to stay that way, and should therefore be left alone. The wall contouring across from the left to meet it however is less well preserved, and its largest gap happens to be here at the junction. Turning down through it, a green path commences a descent in the company of Red Beck, neither of which stray far from the wall. The path becomes stonier in its lower reaches as it drops through trees onto the lakeshore path. Immediately on turning left look up to see the Crag Fell Pinnacles thrusting skyward high up the flanks.

An alternative route breaks off the descending path in its early stages, to offer a rougher but interesting option. To sample it turn off the path to a prominent group of four or five gnarled trees over to the left. Just past them an initially thin path turns half-right down the slope, and as it slants down through heather it soon improves. Discreet cairns perched on boulders help confirm the route, which soon levels off again to traverse the fellside high above the lake. Beyond a gap in a descending wall it runs along as a lovely green track to the grassy col above Anglers' Crag: here one can pick up the lakeshore path either by going through the col to an inviting path slanting down, or turn back down to the right to join the path before it encounters the entertaining crossing of the foot of the crag.

Meanwhile back on the lakeshore path approaching Anglers' Crag one might apprehensively fear an impasse, such is the way the cliffs fall to the water's edge. However a route has been so well worn that only a degree of caution is needed to avoid a slip. Beyond this fascinating tangle the path resumes uneventfully to leave the base of the fell at a stile at the very lakefoot. Across a field a track to the water-gauge house is met to return to the bridge over the river, though a nicer finish crosses the first footbridge to turn down a wooded riverside path to the car park.

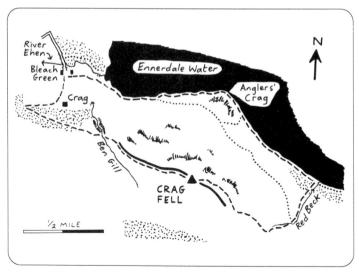

> *Start: Gatesgarth   GR 194149*
> *Maps: 1:25000 - NW; 1:50000 - 89 or 90*
> *4¹⁄2 miles / 1700 feet / 2¹⁄2-3¹⁄2 hours*
> *Parking: Car park opposite farm*

From the car park take the signposted path between the farm buildings, and while crossing the fields beyond, there is ample time to appraise the walk's objective ahead to the left. Haystacks may be surrounded by higher mountains, but it is far from dominated by them. On crossing the bridge over Warnscale Beck, those first easy minutes are soon forgotten as the climb begins in earnest. A footpath sign points the way to 'Ennerdale via Scarth Gap,' and the initially steep section is eased with the aid of zig-zags. Higher up the going eases further and the gentler graded, well worn path slants half-left across the lower flanks of High Crag to gain the green hollow of Scarth Gap. At 1425 feet this is one of the district's lower footpasses, but its setting is as impressive as any.

To the left the final 500 feet of Haystacks await, and a few yards from the cairn the climb recommences. The path rises half-right and within a matter of yards another clear path forks off to the left. The main path continues further before climbing left up a stony shoot, but the early fork is a more pleasant path, and incorporates a simple but enjoyable scramble before they reunite above it. Only a short pull further - during which there is a splendid prospect of the rock tower of Big Stack above Warnscale Bottom - and the summit is reached. The short rocky ridge, cairned at each end, is mirrored in the waters of a classic mountain tarn only feet below the highest ground.

Major features of the view include the great wall of Pillar across Ennerdale, so often brooding in shadow; Great Gable's unmistakable dome at that valley's head, dwarfing its satellite Green Gable; and the most attractive scene, the Buttermere valley stretching away between mountain walls - with High Crag on the left and the delectable Grasmoor group to the right - sheltering both sides of it.

North-west from Haystacks: the Grasmoor Fells rise out of a mist-choked Buttermere valley.

The southernmost cairn on the ridge is marginally the higher, and it is from here that the return path sets forth eastwards across the broad and entirely absorbing main ridge of the fell. The first target in Innominate Tarn, glistening prominently from the summit cairn. Beyond that the path drops down through inspiring surroundings to cross the outflow of Black Beck Tarn, then curves right under the tor of Green Crag before a steady descent towards Dubs Bottom. Across the other side on the slopes of Fleetwith Pike are the conspicuous remains of Dubs Quarry, and indeed the path can be followed right down to the beck and up to the quarry to turn left and descend from there.

The suggested route, however, branches left off the main path before passing beneath the prominent tilted 'training slab' of Little Round How. This path runs past a less obtrusive quarry site to then take advantage of its access track. This descends above the ravine of Warnscale Beck then zig-zags expertly down below Haystacks' menacing cliffs into the sanctuary of Warnscale Bottom, where a footbridge crosses the beck to join the old quarry track from Dubs. The return to Gatesgarth is completed in fine style on a luxurious, level green path. On meeting the Honister road the farm is only a few yards down to the left.

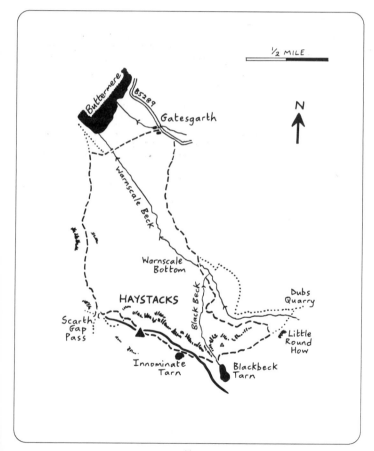

> *Start: Loweswater village*
> *Map: 1:25000 - NW; 1:50000 - 89*
> *6¹/2 miles / 1600 feet / 3-4¹/2 hours*
> *Parking: Only parking in the hamlet is that for*
> *patrons of the inn, with a place for the odd car just*
> *across Church Bridge. There is space for several cars*
> *by the phone box at the road junction*

Leave the staggered crossroads outside the inn by the lane heading south-west to cross Park Beck by Church Bridge. At Kirkgate Farm an unsurfaced lane takes over to rise up to the bottom of a plantation missed by the Ordnance Survey. Here leave the track and climb up the break to gain the open fell. A simple grassy path commences what is clearly going to be a Jekyll and Hyde climb, rising through bracken to the foot of a big scree shoot. A degree of sanity can be retained by taking advantage of the slaty path raking left, which eventually turns to run almost level back to the main path. Above, a rock gateway beckons, but its stony excesses can also be avoided by taking a thinner path left again soon after joining the main path. This slants across to enjoy a splendid moment as it gains a projecting spur with a spectacular craggy face across a deep gully. Throughout the climb, in fact, there are excellent retrospective views embracing the circle of modest fells around Loweswater's basin. Discerning walkers have formed a thin path up this stony rib which will be scaled enthusiastically to once again meet the main path atop the gateway. The path now spirals upwards through dense heather, this second stage of the ascent being broken at a welcome grassy knoll which affords a magical view up the Buttermere valley. Before long the going eases and a short stroll leads to the two cairns on Mellbreak's north top.

Those who have not done their homework will now realise they have not yet climbed Mellbreak, for the true summit of the fell is the south top, a long half-mile away and about ten feet higher. A broad, substantial depression separates the two, and does at least give the opportunity to remain on the heights longer. A path sets off for it, keeping to the right side of the saddle and doing a fine job until the half-way point. At a fork here its intentions become clear as the main branch turns right to descend into Mosedale. The thinner path keeping straight on however will lead almost to the summit of the fell, though fading somewhat before gaining it. A scrappy cairn on the highest ground is usurped by a creditable one a little to the south, the latter being a useful pointer to the line of descent.

Bearing a little to the right of a line of long defunct fenceposts, stride down the grassy flank where a slender trod may or may not be located: it is of little consequence. Aiming for the deep incision of the ravine of Scale Force on the fellside opposite, a minor col is reached before the grassy alp of Scale Knott. Bearing half-right here a fence will be met, and just along to the right a stile is located at a fence junction. At this point the most direct - and driest underfoot - route of return doubles back to the right on the clear path, an uncomplicated trek through Mosedale rejoining the outward path. The main route however crosses the fence and follows the adjoining fence down to another stile and cross-path. Turning left again this attractive path runs above Black Beck, and soon offers a splendid view back to the camera-shy waterfall of Scale Force, a magnificent spectacle.

Having kept its distance the path drops down to the marshy environs of Scale Beck, and beyond a stile accompanies it down towards Crummock Water: note the divergence of the beck, a rare occurrence! In view of the marshy notoriety of this corner of Lakeland, this section is surprisingly dry as a green path runs down through bracken, passing the clearly discernible crumbling walls of an ancient settlement - which in high summer the bracken effectively conceals - indicated on the Ordnance map. Just before the shore the path breaks off to the left, soon gaining the lakeside itself for a prolonged stroll along the base of Mellbreak. The charming peninsula of Low Ling Crag makes a tempting halt, for beyond it a succession of closely grouped marshy tracts rob the walk of full marks. The views across to the resplendent Grasmoor group more than make amends for such minor discomfort, while Mellbreak's craggy frown is constantly above.

At a crumbled wall beyond these interruptions, a solid wall will be seen ahead, and as the route makes for its top corner, take the path rising left to enjoy a level walk well above further quagmires near the foot of the lake. From the wall corner an inviting green path runs along the bottom of a gnarled oakwood, passing above Highpark Farm to a gate at the far corner. Here a walled track runs down to the mini-hamlet of Lowpark and joins a narrow road to cross Park Bridge. A little farther, at another junction, turn left again to return to the inn.

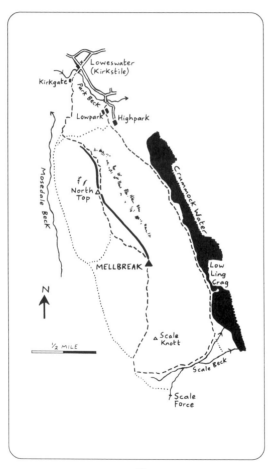

WALK 14   FELLBARROW   1365ft/416m
LOW FELL   1388ft/423m

> *Start: Thackthwaite   GR 148236*
> *Map: 1:25000 - NW; 1:50000 - 89*
> *5¹⁄2 miles / 1500 feet / 2¹⁄2-4 hours*
> *Parking: Extremely limited. There is no space*
> *in the hamlet itself, but room for two or*
> *three cars in a pull-in on the Lorton side*

Leave the hamlet by a rough lane opposite the phone box. It climbs through Thackthwaite Farm and soon becomes a sunken morass, whereupon the path smartly evades it by running up its edge by the field-side. The improving path quickly gains the open fell, and a magnificent drove road sets off to the right. At once there are fine views over Lorton to Hopegill Head's ridges and tops. Again almost at once, after an intervening fence, remain on the green track curving up to the left at a fork. After a short pull to the next fence, the detour to Fellbarrow (the grassy dome across to the right) can be made by rising up the far side of the fence to one on the skyline: turning right from the stile a simple five-minute climb (including another stile) leads to the Ordnance column on Fellbarrow.

Retrace steps to the watershed fence, and on re-crossing the stile do not drop back to the drove road - whose zig-zags above where we left it are plainly in evidence now - but remain with the fence, taking the minor top of Smithy Fell in its stride and descending to a wall at a saddle. Here leave the wall and remain on the slender path cutting across to the left below Sourfoot Fell to rejoin the drove road at another fence. After crossing the stile it is worth continuing left with the fence to inspect the view from the top of Watching Crag before resuming the path's strides to the south. Ahead now the undulating top of Low Fell beckons, and beyond a further fence a little pull leads up onto the crest, marked by a modest pile of stones. Further south still is the slightly lower but more characterful south top, which boasts a fine cairn and an improved view in which Loweswater joins the two other lakes of the Buttermere valley.

After surveying this wondrous prospect return to cross the fence between the two tops, then turn right with it. Although a punishing drop might be expected, only the first section down through the heather is steep, and soon a shelf is reached at the bracken level. Here it is worth locating either of two sheeptrods that slant half-left down the slopes towards the intake fence. Turning left above it a thin path runs along the base of the fell, improving into a delightful green way through the bracken beyond a stile in a fence coming down from the felltop. After passing through a small stand of pines the outward route is regained surprisingly quickly to drop back down to Thackthwaite.

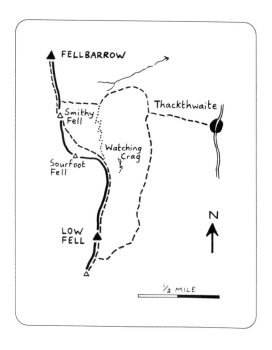

Chapter Three

NORTHERN LAKELAND

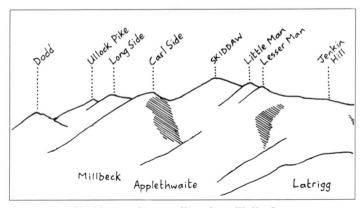

Skiddaw and its satellites from Walla Crag

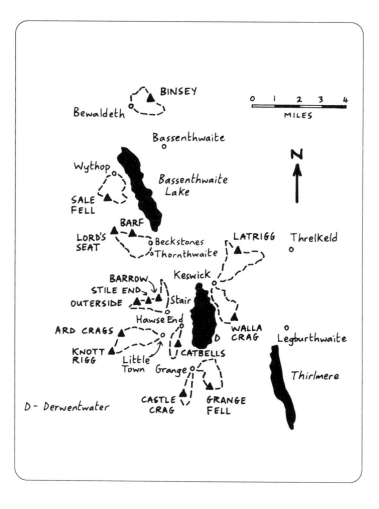

BINSEY

Bewaldeth

Bassenthwaite

0 1 2 3 4
MILES

N

Wythop

Bassenthwaite Lake

SALE FELL

BARF

LORD'S SEAT

Beckstones

Thornthwaite

LATRIGG

Threlkeld

Keswick

BARROW

STILE END

OUTERSIDE

Stair

ARD CRAGS

Hawse End

WALLA CRAG

KNOTT RIGG

Little Town

CATBELLS

Grange

Legburthwaite

Thirlmere

CASTLE CRAG

GRANGE FELL

D - Derwentwater

WALK 15

OUTERSIDE
STILE END
BARROW

1863ft/568m
1466ft/447m
1492ft/455m

Start: Stonycroft, near Stair   GR 232216
Maps: 1:25000 - NW; 1:50000 89 or 90
5¹⁄₂ miles / 1900 feet / 3-4 hours
Parking: Lay-by on the Braithwaite road
north of Stonycroft, above Uzzicar Farm

Opposite the lay-by above Uzzicar, a green bridlepath leaves the road, running south and gaining precious little height above Stonycroft. This splendid route was skilfully constructed to serve a cobalt mine high in the heart of the mountains. Above Stonycroft Bridge the mine road turns to leave the Newlands valley in order to make progress up the side valley of Stonycroft Gill. Over to the left Causey Pike makes first-class viewing while moving steadily up Barrow's colourful flanks.

A little beyond the last tree in the gill, with the flank of Barrow by now receded to a tame heather slope, a cairn indicates the point to leave the mine road if wanting to omit Outerside and Stile End: a slim path doubles back to the right, gravitating marginally uphill to the heather defile of Barrow Door to where the main route will return.

The mine road meanwhile curves up to the left under Outerside's heather cone, to rise to the duller environs of High Moss. At last the track can be vacated to make the short climb up to the right onto Outerside's summit, a seldom frequented top that makes an unrivalled platform for appraising the lofty peaks rimming Coledale. From the cairn a path descends the well defined ridge to the northeast, losing itself somewhat on Low Moss at its foot. Across it the lower eminence of Stile End is soon gained. To reach Barrow Door just beneath it, turn back down to the right to avoid rough slopes and pick up a path curving left to this tidy saddle. At this meeting place of paths, the most popular one heads straight up the broad ridge opposite onto Barrow's summit. A meagre cairn marks this outstanding viewpoint, with the Derwentwater and Vale of Keswick scene balanced by Coledale's brooding mountains.

After such an ascent there is one royal road down, and this is its declining north ridge pointing towards the white walls and grey roofs of Braithwaite. First through heather and then bracken the path runs joyously down, and near the foot of the ridge a wide green crossroads is reached. The right branch doubles back above a plantation to reluctantly rejoin the road along Barrow's base. The starting point is now only a little farther along the broad verged road, beyond a fenced landslip spilling from old mine workings.

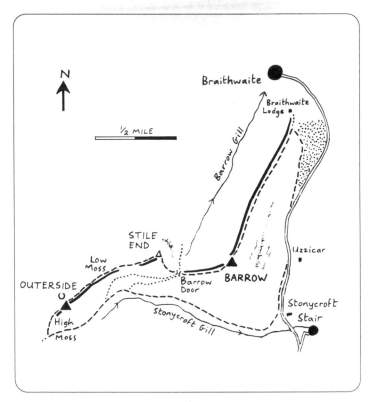

WALK 16   ARD CRAGS   1906ft/581m
             KNOTT RIGG   1824ft/556m

> *Start: Little Town, Newlands*
> *Chapel Bridge   GR 232194*
> *Maps: 1:25000 - NW; 1:50000 - 89 or 90*
> *6¹/2 miles / 1700 feet / 3-4 hours*
> *Parking: Roadside parking on the east*
> *side of Chapel Bridge, to the south*
> *of Little Town*

Cross the bridge and take the winding lane up onto the Newlands Pass road at Rigg Beck. The house here is in its own inimitable way a Lakeland landmark, and it looks down on a hairpin bend where the road crosses the beck. An inviting path heads away along its right bank; up to the right is the serrated top of Causey Pike, and within a minute or so the noble outline of Ard Crags proves equally arresting across the beck. When the wall on the other bank turns away up the slope, descend to cross the beck and rise up to the foot of the exciting looking ridge. A green path climbs through bracken in the traditional pile carpet manner, and as the going steepens heather takes over on the climb to the crest of Aikin Knott. From here on a glorious walk along an exquisite ridge leads to the tiny cairn on Ard Crags.

With a sensational drop immediately to the left from the summit, and classic views of Eel Crag and its lofty fellows to the right, the path continues along the crest to initiate the obvious progression, a traverse to Knott Rigg. In the minor depression grass takes over for the steady rise onto Knott Rigg's less exhilarating summit, the highest point being set some distance back. During this crossing to Knott Rigg the route of descent down Keskadale Edge will be easily located. Having savoured the views over Newlands Pass to the Buttermere valley, turn east from the summit cairn across a small marshy area (note the fenced-off section) to look down the tiny side valley of Ill Gill. Bearing right of it a path materialises to commence a descent of the extremely well defined Keskadale Edge. This little known valley is enclosed by the protective arm of the edge, and the descent over its many undulations is utter delight.

At the foot of the edge bear down to the left to join the road just below Keskadale Farm. After doubling back left to cross Ill Gill, leave the road by a gate on the right, from where a track runs down with the beck to a farm bridge and then a footbridge over Ill Gill and Keskadale Beck respectively. Rising up to the left, the track soon fades for a largely invisible path to run on across the fields above the latter beck, below a compact birchwood and guided by occasional stakes. Contouring round to the right it connects with the High Snab farm road, and turning down it, lonely Newlands church will be passed just before the junction at Chapel Bridge.

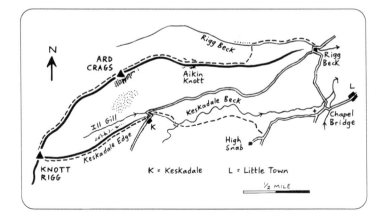

WALK 17   CATBELLS   1479ft/451m

Start: Hawse End   GR 247212
Map: 1:25000 - NW; 1:50000 - 89 or 90
3¹⁄₂ miles / 1250 feet / 2-3 hours
Parking: Below the cattle-grid by the
zig-zags, or in a car park part way
along the farm road to Skelgill

Very little description is needed for this popular walk, which utilises only some of the delectable paths around Catbells. Of all the walks in this book, reserve this one for autumn. From the junction above the cattle-grid turn along the road to Skelgill, continuing past the hamlet on a broad path along the base of the fell. The Newlands valley makes an unforgettable start to the walk, with the Grasmoor group of fells across to the right (Causey Pike most prominent) and Newlands' own mountains directly ahead. A good two-thirds of a mile beyond the farm the first of two paths breaks off to the left - though either can be used - to take its time in breaking away from the level path, eventually rising through part of the former Yewthwaite Mine. The path climbing from Little Town is joined for the short pull to Hause Gate, which is Catbells' link with Maiden Moor and the higher fells. With Derwentwater bursting onto the scene, turn left to follow the path up

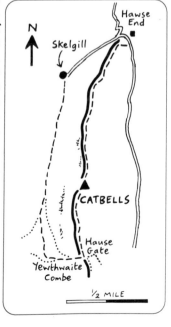

56

the broad ridge to the usually well populated summit.

To return to the valley, continue north along the ridge, on a path that descends enthusiastically over intervening outcrops, and with its views over the lake and the Vale of Keswick, positively defies description. All too soon the foot of the ridge is neared, and the re-routed path turns down to the right to help alleviate the eroded start of the path by the roadside above the junction.

West from Catbells: Rigg Beck penetrates between Ard Crags and the higher level ridge from which Eel Crag spawns Wandope (left), Sail and Scar Crags

WALK 18   CASTLE CRAG   951ft/290m

> *Start: Grange in Borrowdale*
> *Maps: 1:25000 - NW; 1:50000 - 89 or 90*
> *4 miles / 750 feet / 2-3 hours*
> *Parking: Limited space at the bridge*
> *end, or in lay-bys on the main road*
> *towards Keswick*

Leave Grange by a lane heading south out of the village 100 yards away from the bridge, this being the drive to Hollows Farm and bridleway to Honister and Seatoller. Level walking leads to a junction where the farm road swings right and a wide track continues into the woods to join the Derwent. After the second of two inflowing streams a guidepost signals the point to leave the river and take the right fork. At last climbing begins, on the wide track of the old road for Honister.

As height is gained the lofty Goat Crag on High Spy and Castle Crag's own impressive cliffs form mighty portals. As the scree on the left recedes the brow of the old road is approached, but before re-crossing to the right bank of the stream a big cairn on grass signifies the point of departure, by curving up to the top of a small tor on the left. Here will be found a stile in a wall, and a clear path climbs steeply past a memorial seat and stone and up to another wall stile at the foot of scree slopes.

Here are the remains of a slate quarry, and the main path bears right to a cairn at the bottom of a vast spoil heap: it is to this point that steps must be retraced after reaching the summit. A firmly trodden path zig-zags up the mountain of slate in surprisingly easy fashion to arrive at a brace of slate beacons overlooking upper Borrowdale. Behind them is the quarry, with the path climbing to the right to gain the grassy little summit plateau. The highest point is in no doubt, a large mound of rock to which is affixed a war memorial, with the lip of the quarry encroaching dangerously close. While savouring this classic summit, it can easily be envisaged as the British hill fort it once was.

58

On regaining the foot of the great spoil heap, head across the grass to the nearest stile over the adjacent wall, and from it take the path down to the left. It quickly returns to valley level to meet and then turn left with a broad path following the Derwent: almost at once entering thick woodland, a walk in heaven ensues. Although remaining generally close to the river, the main path turns off part way along, and at a junction just past a gateway and spoil heaps there is an opportunity for a short detour up to the left to inspect caves once occupied by one of the district's great characters, Millican Dalton.

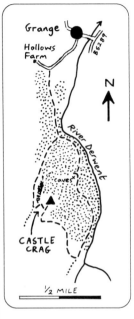

This point can also be reached by a lesser known path that keeps faith with the river longer, being partly a wide green swathe and partly an obstacle course of ponds and outcrops, a veritable wonderland. The main path can be regained by leaving the river at a rock-bound impasse, and turning inland up a curious trough to the spoil heaps at the foot of the caves. Beyond here the re-united path eventually returns to the crystal clear river to rejoin the outward route at the wide bend where it was forsaken to begin the climb.

WALK 19   GRANGE FELL   1345+ft/410+m

Start: Grange in Borrowdale
Maps: 1:25000 - NW; 1:50000 - 89 or 90
6 miles / 1400 feet / 3-4 hours
Parking: Limited space in the village
at the bridge end, with lay-bys on the
main road towards Keswick

Leave Grange by crossing the twin bridge over the Derwent and turning right along the road. Just beyond the large house a stile admits to the bracken clad fell, and a thin path heads away, keeping left. Bear left again then right to join a wider path out of the hollow, leading up to a brow, through a gate and down to a fork. Ignoring the left branch to a stile, the right arm drops down to cross a tiny stream to begin a long climb through the beautifully wooded slopes of King's How, westernmost and lower of Grange Fell's two main tops.

Occasional glimpses of Derwentwater can be stolen while pausing, then suddenly the going eases and the work is done. The path runs along towards a fence, but instead of crossing it, rises alongside it to the edge of Long Moss hidden between heathery knolls. Skirting it to the right the path then climbs again, presenting panoramic views into Borrowdale, with a glimpse of Grange itself before the last pull to the scattered summit cairn. Just below the highest point a tablet affixed to the rock records in fine words the gift of King's How to the nation.

'In Loving Memory of King Edward VII Grange Fell is dedicated by his sister Louise as a sanctuary of rest and peace. Here may all beings gather strength, and find in scenes of beautiful nature a cause for gratitude and love to God giving them courage and vigour to carry on his will'.

To the south-east Brund Fell, true summit of Grange Fell makes its superiority clear. To reach it retrace steps a few yards to the tiny cairned saddle just below, and here take the path to the right. It drops steeply to skirt the top end of Long Moss to the fence which can finally

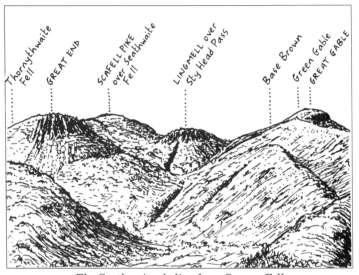

The Seathwaite skyline from Grange Fell

be crossed. The path continues on to an intervening wall, and shortly after a slight rise beyond a ruined fold, a branch bearing up to the left is taken. Here the path from Rosthwaite is joined for the final climb onto the summit. The highest of several tors is crowned by a cairn: while this top has much more interest than King's How, it forfeits the magnificent view of Derwentwater.

The main path off the top resumes the direction of the ascent, winding down to a stile in the nearby wall corner. Heading directly away, the path encounters marshy ground during a descent to Watendlath that conceals the tarn and its attendant white cottages almost until the very last minute. When they do appear, and in style, a short drop leads down to the outflow of the tarn. This is a charming place for a potter about, and on leaving it is necessary to re-cross the bridge to a gate adjacent to it. After only a few yards in the company of the lively beck, the path is ushered away by a wall to run along the base of the fell. In time the water's edge is rejoined, and a lovely stroll concludes in glorious woodland at a footbridge.

Without crossing the bridge, note the novel footpath sign and go left to a wicket gate into the edge of Ashness Wood. The beck is briefly encountered again in the midst of some sudden changes of direction and a ferociously thundering fall through a gorge, before the path keeps onto a collapsed wall. From this low saddle a short detour should be made along the path to the right, which rises onto the colourful top of Shepherds Crag. This is a near island of rock, and has an excellent view of Gowder Crag across the now deep rift of Watendlath Beck. Back at the saddle, with Borrowdale now laid out in front, the path makes the short descent of Ladder Brow to return to the valley by way of High Lodore Farm. Turning left, the footpath along the roadside will be gratefully accepted as a reasonably safe means of returning to Grange.

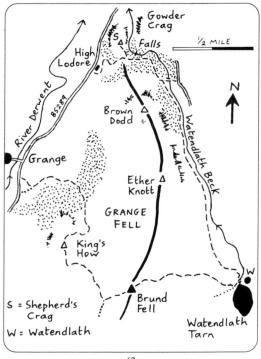

> *Start: Keswick on Derwentwater boat landings*
> *Map: 1:25000 - NW; 1:50000 - 89 or 90*
> *5¹⁄2 miles / 1050 feet / 2¹⁄2-4 hours*
> *Parking: The large Lakeside car park*

From Derwentwater's boat landings immediately forsake the lakeside road in favour of a path into the woodland just past the National Trust kiosk. There turn right along a wide path curving round through Cockshot Wood, emerging at the other side to run between fields out onto the Borrowdale road. Straight across a wicket gate gives access to Castlehead Wood, first rising steeply towards a brow before a branch up to the right to the crown of Castle Head. A mere 531 feet above sea level, this is arguably Derwentwater's finest viewpoint, certainly for the effort involved. High above the lake to the left is the brooding frame of Walla Crag, looking far larger than it really is, and belying the ease by which its top will be gained. Returning to the path junction, continue along to the right, descending to the edge of the wood and out along another enclosed path onto a road.

Turn right along Springs Road to the end of the suburban row, and at Springs Farm bear left on a profusely signposted path that climbs above the wooded charms of Brockle Beck. At the top the beck is crossed by a footbridge to rise onto a narrow lane. Go right to its imminent demise at Rakefoot, keeping right at the fork (where Walla Crag earns its own road sign) to pass outside the confines of the farm. A small footbridge re-crosses the beck to a path climbing by the wall-side, and through a stile the open fell is reached. Remaining with the wall throughout, it is but a gentle grassy pull onto Walla Crag. The drama will unfold rapidly as the wall is crossed at the first chance (a wicket gate) to cautiously follow the edge of the clifftops. Leaving the last of the trees the path runs to a cairn standing on the highest point, just yards back from the alarmingly abrupt escarpment. The breath-taking panorama over the expanse of Derwentwater is guaranteed to demand a substantial break in the journey.

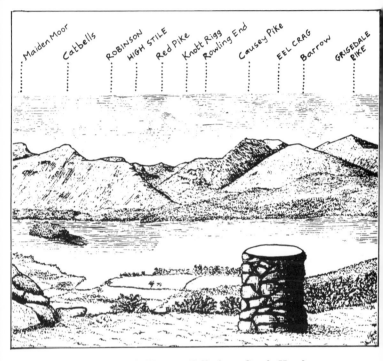

Maiden Moor · Catbells · ROBINSON · HIGH STILE · Red Pike · Knott Rigg · Rowling End · Causey Pike · EEL CRAG · Barrow · GRISEDALE PIKE

The North-Western Fells from Castle Head

From the summit continue along the path heading south, which within a couple of minutes re-crosses the wall at a stile. Continue down by the wall on a short cropped green carpet, a path that undergoes a drastic character change as the environs of Cat Gill are entered. The ground steepens rapidly and the path begins a winding descent towards the Borrowdale road, with much essential restoration work having rendered the path far more bearable. At the foot of the steeper section Great Wood is briefly entered, only to leave it again by way of a footbridge over the beck. Back out on bracken cloaked lower slopes, a path runs down by the wall to a stile onto the road. A little more pleasure can be derived by taking the level path away from the bridge to appraise the mighty cliff of Falcon Crag up to the left: at the first opportunity then take a green path down to the right to the stile onto the road, which can be crossed straight over to Derwentwater's shore.

Turning right along the lakeshore, a finish that does justice to the rest of the walk is now in store. In and out of woodland the path curves round Calfclose Bay, being diverted briefly away from the lake by the house at Stable Hills. Following its drive away, at the first opportunity it is escaped on a well trodden path to the left to run through trees. The shore is regained in time to reach the famous peninsula of Friar's Crag, from where it is but a few hundred heavily populated yards back to the boat landings, and the ice cream and the ducks, and....

WALK 21   LATRIGG   1207ft/368m

Start: Keswick
Maps: 1:25000 - NW; 1:50000 - 89 or 90
6¹⁄2 miles / 900 feet / 2¹⁄2-4 hours
Parking: Several car parks, or limited
space on the route itself on Briar
Rigg, west of Spooney Green Lane

Leave the Moot Hall in the market place by way of St. John's Street, Station Street and Station Road, and once across the river turn left into Fitz Park. Crossing to the far corner, a footpath escapes to emerge onto the back road of Briar Rigg. Turn right a short distance to where Spooney Green Lane leaves opposite the houses to climb at once to bridge the by-pass, a scene inconceivable not that very long ago. Sanity is restored as it climbs past Thorny Plats and up by a plantation. The steepness soon recedes here, never to return. Opportunities to strike out more positively for Latrigg's summit soon present themselves with regularity, but they should all be refused in favour of the main highway with its views across to Skiddaw. To forsake this fair track would not be playing the game.

As the plantation on the right fades, one on the left soon takes over, and above it, a second, more extensive one adjoins the path. Ever broad, and a delight to walk, the path is finally vacated well along the plantation, vigilance being needed to locate the even more inviting green path that doubles back to the right. In the tradition of this ascent it zigzags famously up through receding bracken - now it is clear why we waited for it! - before rising across to the western end of what constitutes Latrigg's summit ridge. Keswick lies outspread below, though the picture of Derwentwater and Borrowdale beyond is a big improvement on the streets and roofs. A substantial mound now leads up to the felltop, which has no cairn and is decidedly arbitrary but nevertheless thoroughly wonderful.

Continuing along the edge, the mound runs along to its demise at a fence, and from the stile there a green path sets off for a gradual descent of Latrigg's east ridge. A long way further it is deflected left to join a green track, which is the continuation of the Gale Road that ends its surfaced life on the northern slope of Latrigg. This takes over to continue down the ridge to descend through gorse to a junction of back roads. The right branch gives a return to Keswick through Brundholme Woods, while that curving round to the left leads only to Lonscale Farm. Instead, go left a few yards and take the road descending past Brundholme to an arched bridge over Glenderaterra Beck.

Without crossing the bridge, a short path runs to the old Penrith-Keswick railway line, which provides a novel return to the start. Turning right, it commences a remarkable journey through the wooded gorge of the river Greta, re-crossing the tumbling waters on several occasions and providing alternatives that head off into the woods. The old track bed was purchased and transformed into a walkers' route by the National Park Authority, but even their imaginative efforts couldn't cope with the intrusion of the Keswick by-pass. Just beyond the caravans at the former bobbin mill at Briery (note the old platform), a rare and spectacular viewpoint opens out, looking upstream towards Blencathra, and straight across the river to the steep flanks of Latrigg, where it is gratifying to note the abysmal if not unexpected failure of the plantings on the highest slopes.

This point marks a brief departure, not from the line, but of the line. The embankment of the by-pass has obliterated the course of the railway, and a climb to the edge of the pulsating highway is an alarming moment prior to the realisation that it doesn't have to be crossed. The path runs down to the right to pass under the road at the commencement of its sweeping concrete crossing high above the Greta. So often a jarring note in views across the Vale of Keswick, these experiences will be cast into irrelevance after this mind-numbing experience. Awe-inspiring it may be, but it is also unquestionably the most horrendous sight in the entire National Park.

On the other side the track bed returns, suddenly now very much on the urban edge of Keswick. It nevertheless gives an interesting route into the town, passing over the main road and adjacent river to chug into the restored station (closed 1972), where one can eat, drink, and obtain timeshare information. In view of the demise of the Cockermouth, Keswick and Penrith Railway this tarting up seems incongruous; insulting even, by the time a sign pointing to a 'brasserie' is reached. To return to the centre double back down onto the road to pass under the old line and back up between the parks into the town, or for Briar Rigg keep straight on to the roundabout where this complex meets the road, and turn left along sanity restoring Briar Rigg, with its glorious view across to Skiddaw.

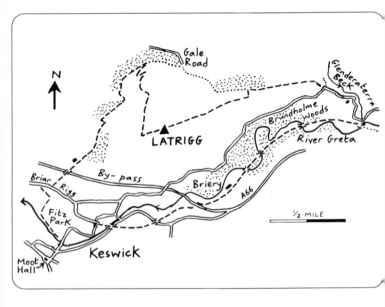

WALK 22   BARF   1535ft/468m
              LORD'S SEAT   1811ft/552m

> *Start: Beckstones   GR 220264*
> *(1 mile north of Thornthwaite off A66)*
> *Map: 1:2500 - NW; 1:50000 - 89 or 90*
> *5½ miles / 1700 feet / 2½-4 hours*
> *Parking: Forestry Commission car park at*
> *Powter How, north of the Swan Hotel*

From the green outside the Swan Hotel a narrow road sets off through the trees across the former main road. It crosses Beckstones Gill to the house at Beckstones, but once over the bridge it can be vacated at a stile on the right. A good path climbs by the beck to eventually submerge itself in the trees of Beckstones Plantation. During the lower part of the climb there are ample opportunities to appraise the wild face of Barf across the beck, and in particular to locate its whitewashed Bishop. This famous cleric is a long established landmark in these parts, and a rather less civilised route from the roadside trees could be engaged to incorporate his slaty self in a direct ascent for the roughnecks.

Back in the plantation meanwhile, height is gained with less difficulty as glimpses of the heathery flanks of Barf show its aggressiveness to be rapidly receding. Excitement is provided by a minor scramble up a band of rock across the path. On meeting a second forest road, this one does not merely cease like the first, but turns uphill on our route up the edge of the plantation. Almost at once however it can be vacated by making for a prominent stile in the fence. Suddenly outside the trees, a charming path re-crosses Beckstones Gill and makes its way joyously up gentle slopes to Barf's grassy top.

After consuming the majestic prospect of the Skiddaw group rising beyond the vast waters of Bassenthwaite, steps can turn to the undemanding slopes in the opposite direction, where the grassy dome of Lord's Seat beckons. An obvious path heads off, making directly for the intervening depression before a climb that involves an unexpected disappointingly boggy tract before the final pull. Two forlorn straining posts occupy the windy top, and this hierarch of the Whinlatter fells offers views appropriate to its status.

The route of departure is south, towards the extensive plantations that together form Whinlatter Forrest. The forest fence runs only a short distance below the summit dome, and the right-hand of two stiles is the one to choose. From it a newly constructed path heads away, and like it or not one must concede it makes light work of the marshy terrain. Running casually through the heather in the direction of the tree-free Ullister Hill ahead, there is clearly no haste to plunge into the forest proper. At two junctions our chosen route bears left each time, passing curious pockets of conifers before turning more sharply left to soon drop down into the inevitable: the terminus of a forest road is reached, and the well made track can be followed along to the right. Numbers in brackets hereon relate to forest marker posts, which make useful guides.

So begins a prolonged descent through Beckstones Plantation, the upper half of which accompanies forest roads that decline ever cautiously to facilitate the passage of vehicles. This first section of forest road is followed gently down for about three-quarters of a mile, and long after passing two roads doubling back to the left (7 & 8), a wide junction (9) is reached. With a wide gap in the trees permitting a fine prospect of Causey Pike straight ahead, turn left to double back down a hairpin bend, and down to another junction (11) where this time the northern ridges of Grisedale Pike are neatly revealed (the road going left ends at the rock band on the ascent). Only a handful of yards along to the right however, an innocuous green path slopes off from this abnormally wide road, a little gem that slants down to become a track and crosses Comb Gill. Before the next tiny beck and nearby junction (13) with a climbing road, take another path striking down to the left.

Passing a diminutive stone enclosure across the beck, it re-crosses Comb Gill where a wider path comes in to slant away from it. This pleasant path drops down to meet a forest road which it happily crosses straight over to soon make acquaintance with tumbling Comb Beck. In idyllic surroundings, like woodland was meant to be, it is shadowed down to a gate out of the woods, a novel entry onto a narrow lane leading past white houses to emerge onto a back road in Thornthwaite. Turning left and keeping left, the road runs above the village to join the main road through it. The Swan Hotel is now only minutes further, and this already quiet road can be left by a road to the left after the last house to finish by way of the start, at Beckstones. A prize feature of the concluding half-mile is a fine prospect of Barf.

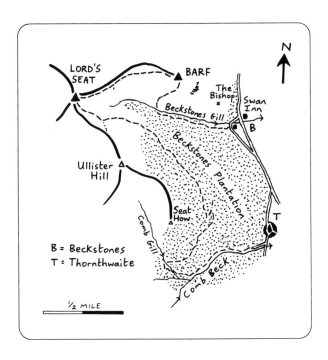

> *Start: Pheasant Inn, Wythop   GR 199306*
> *Map: 1:25000 - NW sheet and Pathfinders*
> *575 NY 03/13, 576 NY 23/33*
> *(neither worth buying specially)*
> *1:50000 - 89 or 90*
> *4¹⁄₂ miles / 1000 feet / 2-3 hours*
> *Parking: On the wide road near the inn,*
> *bypassed by the modern A66*

From the junction by the inn take the road signposted to Wythop Mill, rising steadily past several dwellings until just short of Wythop Church on the brow, a wicket-gate is seen on the left. From it a path slants up through the field to a similar gate onto the open fell (note the white cross on a rock above during the climb). Just above the gate is a terrace path, which is followed right to the brow on Sale Fell's west ridge. Forsaking the faint but broad path, a slender one breasts the grassy ridge, though almost at once it is worth bearing right a little off its lightly trodden course to take in the crest of the colourful outcrops of Dodd Crag above the secluded Wythop valley. Keeping to the height of land the lightweight green track is regained to attain the noteworthy summit cairn.

The next objective is the grassy shelf of Lothwaite, in the direction of Bassenthwaite Lake to the east. Incomparably easy walking resumes as the path runs down the slope, through two well collapsed walls and bears left below a cairned top to a little col: here a thinner path takes up the running to rise up to the left to Lothwaite's tiny cairn. The already memorable view of Skiddaw and its ridges beyond the lake is now surpassed with the addition of depth of foreground.

Continuing the remaining way along the ridge to the proud oaks on the edge of Wythop Woods, a short descent to the right will meet a broad green track as it enters the forest. Making use of it, only a few yards in it meets the hairpin of a forest road. A typically dawdling descent now ensues, it being some time before the first opportunity to turn downhill arises. Remaining on the main track it zigzags down through several junctions, taking the downhill branch at each turn. At a particularly major junction a splendid open prospect over the lake to Skiddaw greets the eye, and turning down to the left the administrative centre of Thornthwaite Forest is reached. From here a surfaced drive leads out onto the road on which the walk began, just short of the inn.

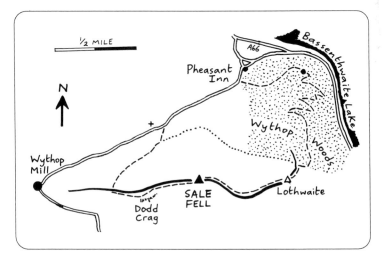

> *Start: Bewaldeth   GR 209347*
> *Map: 1:25000 - Pathfinder 576 NY23/33*
> *1:50000 - 89 or 90*
> *4¹/2 miles / 1000 feet / 2-3 hours*
> *Parking: Room on the verges of the slip*
> *road to the village off the A591*

Head north along the main road with its ample grass verge, and after a quarter mile turn right up a green track through an avenue of trees pointing away from a gate. It gains height only steadily until reaching the open fell: look out for hang-gliders taking off from the grassy slopes over to the left. A short-lived track rises half-left across the fell to the grassed over gravel pit it once served, and from here sketchy trods, at best, can be traced up the heather slopes to the right onto the bouldery crest of West Crag. This modest portion of rough terrain is Binsey's only such roughness, and cannot be mistaken. A thin path then runs on through a shallow trough, used by farm vehicles, to gain the summit of the fell.

The felltop is in fact a short ridge, on which have been constructed an Ordnance column, a cairn, and a great pile of boulders given antiquity status, with a more modern shelter incorporated. The way off returns to the farmer's track in the trough and resumes its course to the south-east, with the secluded tarn of Over Water a good guide in front of the Uldale Fells. The track remains distinct until it leaves the heather zone, but the belt of trees around Binsey Lodge will by then be located, and the subdued path continues down to emerge onto a back road by way of some sheep pens. The road junction outside the derelict lodge is just yards to the left, but the return route turns immediately right to accompany the narrow road all the way back down to Bewaldeth. Although this is quite a lengthy spell on tarmac, it is virtually traffic-free, is downhill all the way, rural, peaceful, and affords excellent views over the fields to a sizeable expanse of the silvery waters of Bassenthwaite Lake, with the Skiddaw massif rising across to the left.

The ascent of Binsey from the west

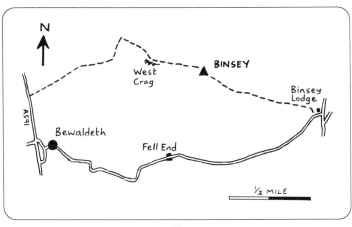

Chapter Four

EASTERN LAKELAND

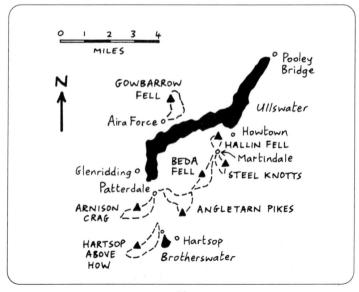

West from Angle Tarn: the lofty peaks across the Patterdale valley

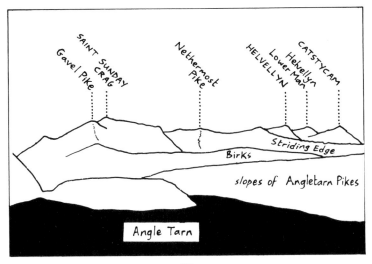

Gavel Pike

SAINT SUNDAY CRAG

Nethermost Pike

HELVELLYN

Lower Man

Helvellyn

CATSTYCAM

Striding Edge

Birks

slopes of Angletarn Pikes

Angle Tarn

WALK 25   GOWBARROW FELL   1578ft/481m

> *Start: Park Brow Foot, Ullswater*
> *(Aira Force car park)*
> *Maps: 1:25000 - NE; 1:50000 - 90*
> *4¹₂ miles / 1100 feet / 2-3 hours*
> *Parking: National Trust car park*
> *on A592 near junction with A5091*

Leave the car park by the bustling path at its far end, which soon dives into the trees. Bear right shortly after on the path down to a wooden footbridge over Aira Beck, and keep right when the path up the other side forks. Only yards further the heavy waterfall traffic can be escaped completely by bearing right again to a stile in a fence onto the open fell, just beyond which another clear path heads along to the right. Running briefly along the base of Gowbarrow Fell, with Ullswater down to the right, another fork is soon reached: here take the inviting path slanting up to the left, which proves an effortless means of gaining height while also extending the outstanding views over the lake (note the novel shape of the shooting lodge of Lyulph's Tower immediately below). The path soon levels out and contours along the southern flank of the fell to arrive at a distant corner, where a prominent cairn just to the right stands high above Yew Crag and begs a visit.

From here the path swings around to the left and maintains its undemanding course, now traversing the fell's eastern flank again in grand style. This section ends at a decaying shooting box just before a wall, across which, incidentally, is a delectable picnic spot by a tinkling stream. Without taking the inviting stile, our route turns up to the left on a path that rises above the wall and a tiny beck, passing gradually from bracken to the upper heather zone. A little damp higher up, the path concludes with a pull up to the left to gain the distinct summit of the fell. An Ordnance column adorned with a National Trust sign doubly confirms the location.

While the fells around Blencathra to the north-west and the

The head of Ullswater from the cairn above Yew Crag

Martindale district across the lake are well seen, the intimate picture of the lake itself is not available from this location. To rectify this, turn south along the broad, heathery and occasionally marshy ridge, one of several winding trods being made use of to ease the journey. As grassier terrain takes over, a better path forms to run along to a conspicuous cairn on Green Hill, virtually at the ridge-end. Here a pleasant discovery is made in the shape of a broad green path, which turns to the right to take us down in the precise direction required. The whole descent is a total joy, the view of the upper reaches of the lake backed by the Helvellyn range matching up to the quality of the path underfoot.

At the bottom a fence is reached, and just along to the left is a gate only yards along from the stile where we first gained the fellside. To complete the walk in the appropriate manner, turn right along the path to Aira Force. Just before the waterfall it forks to provide an opportunity to view the spectacle from a tiny arched bridge above, then returning down the path to the bridge at the foot of the fall for the more conventional view. The lower path heading back downstream can now be taken to return to the bridge at the outset of the walk, retracing the first few hundred yards or so back to the car park.

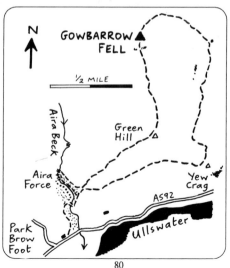

WALK 26 ANGLETARN PIKES 1860ft/567m

Start: Patterdale
Maps: 1:25000 - NE; 1:50000 - 90
4¹⁄₂ miles / 1450 feet / 2¹⁄₄-3 ¹⁄₂ hours
Parking: Car park in the village

Patterdale is left by the access road branching left over Goldrill
Bridge, beyond the White Lion Hotel at the Kirkstone end of the
village. Bearing round to the left, the road ends at a complex of gates,
with one on the right (Angle Tarn and Boredale Hause) granting
access to the open fell. The much trodden path slants up to the right,
and at an early fork the lower one is appropriate, the higher being
used in the return. With implicit ease the path gains height to meet
a green track from Hartsop just below a sheepfold. This location could
almost be known as the lower Boredale Hause, for it is the nearest
many walkers come to the true pass, which is just up to the left.

The path to Angletarn Pikes and so many other wonderful places
crosses the beck just above the fold and heads upwards again, never
faltering as it runs through a narrow trough to emerge above the
ravine of Dubhow Beck, with its magnificent views over Brotherswater
to the Kirkstone fells, and across the main valley to the great bowl of
Deepdale. Here the path makes a distinct fork, and while either will
lead to Angle Tarn, it is important to take the upper one when bound
for the Pikes. After a short level stroll a cairn is met just before the
brow of this path, and here it is time to strike up the grassy slope to
the castellated North top of Angletarn Pikes. Some care is needed here
as the airy peak has a craggy fall to the south. The slightly lower South
top rises across a depression, and should be visited if only for the birds-
eye view of Angle Tarn which the main summit fails to deliver.

The temptation to wander down to the tarn may be strong, and can
easily be incorporated into the walk. If the weather should have
turned for the worse, then it is in any case probably advisable to take
in the tarn and then return by the outward route. The main route,
meanwhile, leaves either of the two Pikes by heading east, each top

Angletarn Pikes from the foot of Coldcove Gill in Deepdale
(Walk 27)

offering a slender trod to weave through grassy alps to come upon a
previously visible path rising from the vicinity of the tarn. Turning
left along it the way is clear again, the path skirting round the back
of Heck Crag, which merits a visit for its dramatic headlong view down
Bannerdale. Also worth remembering to seek out is the retrospective
view of the Pikes' main top, which assumes a remarkable tor-like
outline for a short spell.

Beyond this point the ridge takes shape for its long journey out to
Beda Fell. On this occasion however it is vacated a short distance after
a very prominent cairn, where the Bannerdale-Boredale Hause
bridleway crosses the ridge. It can be joined without going to the cairn
at the very junction, for it will be seen to double back to the left at an
acute angle before this. The excellent path slants cautiously across
the fellside, crossing Freeze Beck and coming down to the wide saddle
of Boredale Hause. Instead of trending left to rejoin the outward path,
take a thin trod for the summit of the pass where another ruin can be
seen.

Although the ruin appears to be an old fold, it is in fact the remains of a chapel. From it a path turns left for Patterdale, sloping steadily down a few yards to a conspicuous cairn at the commencement of the fellside's steep drop. Here the descent proper begins, now on the higher of the two outward paths, from where it can now be appreciated how each is more relevant to its own particular goal. Magnificent views over the head of Ullswater and into the side valley of Glenridding with its attendant peaks are good reason to slow down this all too rapid return to the valley floor. At the bottom further variety can be added by turning right along the farm road to Side Farm and then going left along its access road back into Patterdale.

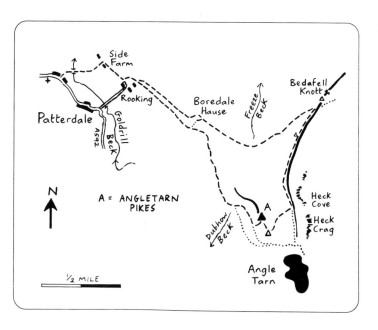

> Start: Patterdale
> Maps: 1:25000 - NE; 1:50000 - 90
> 4 miles / 1000 feet / 2-3 hours
> Parking: Car park in the village

Leave Patterdale by the public footpath signposted up the rough road by the White Lion car park, passing the toilets and curving up to a garage. Behind the garage fork left (for Grisedale), passing Mill Moss and the rear of the Patterdale Hotel. From this level path Arnison Crag rises immediately up to the left. On reaching a wall do not go through the gate with the path, but begin the climb by taking the path rising steeply with the wall. It remains close to it for most of the ascent until the wall eventually swings away to the right. Continue uphill, and before reaching the summit the path fades and itself heads off to the right. By this stage however, only a short pull is needed to gain the characterful top. Two rocky tors, each cairned, mark the summit, the main one being guarded by a craggy wall.

Arnison Crag excels as a viewpoint for the Patterdale valley, with Ullswater stretching away at one end and Hartsop and its environs sheltering beneath the Kirkstone fells at the other. Westwards the high mountains of the Fairfield group present an imposing scene, and this is the direction in which to head. A steep drop resumes the walk, to a depression from where a thin trod heads away towards the next knoll, which is in fact marginally higher than that which has fittingly been conferred the summit. Beyond this top the most slender of trods weaves on along the grassy crest, with the wall still some way down to the right. The ridge ends at a pronounced dog-leg bend where the flanks of Birks start a climb up to the right, with Saint Sunday Crag directly ahead.

At this point even the trod fades away, and the short descent commences by striking out in the direction of the domes of Dove Crag and Hart Crag across Deepdale, restraining the decline to a very gradual one while aiming for the tree lined Coldcove Gill directly ahead. If it is reached at the right place it will be crossed with ease, preferably at a break in the trees above a waterfall into a ravine. A path materialises to descend the far bank, running down a grassy tongue before crossing the side beck also, to join a green path. This works down through bracken in a wonderful manner, with the tinkling beck the only company one needs.

All too soon the track up Deepdale is met at a ruinous enclosure. Turning left it soon becomes an access track, and leads unerringly back past several habitations, including Deepdale Hall, to emerge onto the main road south of the village. This final section along the road is provided with an adjacent footpath which is unable to decide which side of the road it prefers.

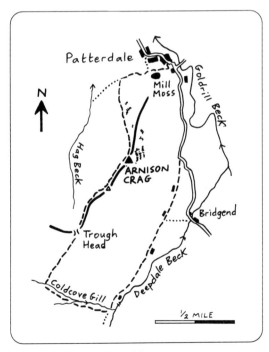

WALK 28   HARTSOP ABOVE HOW
1903+ft/580+m

> *Start: Brotherswater   GR 402133*
> *Map: 1:25000 - NE; 1:50000 - 90*
> *6 miles / 1400 feet / 3·4 hours*
> *Parking: Cow Bridge car park, on the main*
> *road at the northern end of Brotherswater*

At the corner of the car park a gate admits to a broad track to Hartsop
Hall Farm: use the gate, but instead of following the track (our return
route) the walk begins by turning right along a permissive path
through the bottom of the wood, parallel with but avoiding the busy
road. At the end it emerges onto the road for a few yards, and just over
the brow take a stile (Fairfield via Hoggill Brow) on the left. Indefinite
as it is, this is the start of the Hartsop above How ridge. The ascent
begins by bearing left to the wall and fence, where an intermittent
path climbs through the trees of Deepdale Park. The short-lived fence
is soon replaced by a wall, which the route is to follow for the most part
of the climb.

As the trees are left behind early views are gleaned of the fells that
will dominate the climb, Saint Sunday Crag and Fairfield enclosing
Deepdale. Further to the right of the wall a clearer path forms, though
it matters little in this uncomplicated grassy climb. At a stile in a
surprise intervening wall, look over the adjacent stile for a spectacular birds-eye view of Hartsop. On the brow above, the rest of the ridge
climbing to the summit appears, with parent fell Hart Crag behind.
Eventually the wall departs, though only grudgingly dropping away
to the left. Ahead now, on topping a prominent knoll with a fine view
of the Kirkstonefoot area, the broad grassy ridge runs along to narrow
just prior to the top.

By now the aspect of Dove Crag rising above its valley dominates
to the left, and in Dovedale itself the path to which the walk shall
descend can be clearly discerned. A marked cleft above precipitous
Gill Crag precedes arrival on the top of Hartsop above How, where a

six-inch high cairn sits on a minor outcrop, a perfect backrest for the purpose of viewing Dove Crag, Hart Crag and Fairfield. The grandest scene is the head of Dovedale, a very complete picture.

The thought of a descent to the left is certain to instil apprehension, and on no account should it be commenced until following the ridge down to the marshy depression ahead. Here, exactly at its lowest point, turn down the entirely grassy flank to the waiting path. From saddle to path the rapidly accomplished loss of height is only 700 feet, though it might be advisable - perhaps unavoidable - to sit down once or twice to savour the delights of the Dove Crag scene. As the path is neared the bracken zone is reached and the gradient eases.

Turning left on the path along the flank of Hartsop above How, our not inconsiderable altitude provides us with a splendid terrace for appraising the Dovedale landscape. In time the path passes the site of lead mines and drops down to a barn complex to run along to Hartsop Hall Farm. Forking left behind the farm, a pleasant track makes for the heavily wooded base of the fell, running along the length of Brotherswater to return to the car park.

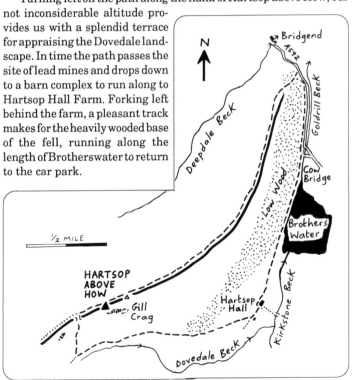

WALK 29   STEEL KNOTTS   1417ft/432m
HALLIN FELL   1273ft/388m

Start: Martindale Hause   GR 435191
Map: 1:25000 - NE; 1:50000 - 90
4 miles / 1400 feet / 2-3 hours
Parking: On the summit of the
hause by St. Peter's Church

This colourful pairing offer a wonderful insight into the Martindale scene, and though they could be climbed almost as easily on separate occasions, combined they form a more worthwhile expedition. From the road top take the path up past the church onto the open fell behind, where the pool of Lanty Tarn is located just across from the wall. It is backed by a line of crags that are circumvented on the right to climb a small gully. The grassy north-west rib of the fell with its attractive outcrops of rock is soon scaled, the gradients easing at a cairn. Merging with the main ridge a straightforward stroll ensues along the crest, the highest point sitting some distance further south and rendered unmistakable by virtue of the solid tor rejoicing in the name of Pikeawassa occupying its highest point.

Though Hallin Fell stands to the north, the route continues south along the broadening ridge to descend towards a wall corner. At the wall the ridge can be vacated by dropping down with it to meet a path doubling back to the right. This splendid way slants down the fellside to a large enclosure, here branching left to descend to the road alongside Martindale Old Church (St. Martin's). Going left to cross Howe Grain Beck by Christy Bridge, the road is then left by turning up the side of Wintercrag. A slate sign points the way to a walled green track running along the rear of the farm buildings.

With Hallin Fell filling the picture ahead, the track runs on to emerge onto the Sandwick road above Howe Grain Beck. Turn down to cross the bridge then go immediately left along a drive to Hallin

Bank. Within yards the wall starts to climb away, and should be accompanied on a green path up through bracken. A level path will be crossed but the way continues up, and when the wall turns right, a second level path will be joined. Turn right along this trod, above the intake wall to meet the broad green swathe of the popular Hallin Fell climb from the hause. Turning up it, the magnificently constructed summit beacon will be gained all too soon.

A variation return to the hause can be made by taking the path heading north-east, which swings back round to the right to cross to the conspicuous Howtown cairn. From here a green path keeps above the craggy Howtown flank and is soon back in familiar surroundings to descend to the road top.

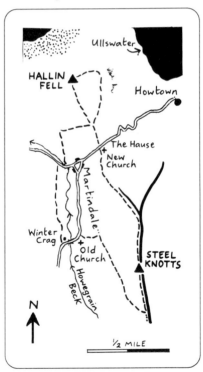

WALK 30   BEDA FELL   1670ft/509m

> Start: Martindale Old Church   GR 434183
> Maps: 1:25000 - NE; 1:50000 - 90
> 5 miles / 1250 feet / 2¹/4-3¹/2 hours
> Parking: Tidily on the roadside

From the old church of St. Martin cross Christy Bridge over Howe Grain Beck and then leave the road by turning up the fellside by Wintercrag. Already Beda Fell is underfoot, and the path to take is a slowly forming one climbing with a crumbling wall on the right, in preference to the more obvious green track running along behind the farm buildings. Within minutes the path gains Beda Fell's ridge at a green crossroads above its northern terminus, and its uncomplicated ascent commences. Almost immediately the path confronts the finest feature of the ridge, the knobbly crest of Winter Crag, then settles down to a steady climb. Two paths rise from the depression beyond, and though there is little to choose, the left one, staying more on the edge, is the usual route. As more height is gained a prominent beacon proves, as expected, not to be the summit, and the slim path actually keeps it on the other side of a marshy depression before the final pull to the summit cairn.

Of the many charming aspects of the Martindale area, the prospect of The Nab, in the heart of the secluded deer forest, is as fair as any. Having climbed to this altitude there is now no rush to lose it all, and the path heading off along the grassy ridge-top can be taken up. After a marshy tract just behind the summit the path settles down to a relaxing, undulating trod, with Heck Crag and Angletarn Pikes occupying the ridge farther on. Long before these heights, however, the ridge is to be vacated by means of a transverse path linking Bannerdale and Boredale Hause. A little surprisingly it does not cross the ridge at its lowest point, but a short way up the other side. Having barely gained any appreciable height beyond the lowest point, the ridge path comes up against the rocky bluff of Bedafell Knott, and here the path forks. The left branch cleverly evades the pull by contouring along to join the aforementioned return path, which can be seen from the fork.

This cross-path is met at a ruin, and a glance uphill to appraise its classic engineered course can be made before turning for home on the broad, slanting descent to Bannerdale. At Dale Head Farm its access road is joined for a traffic free journey back to the church.

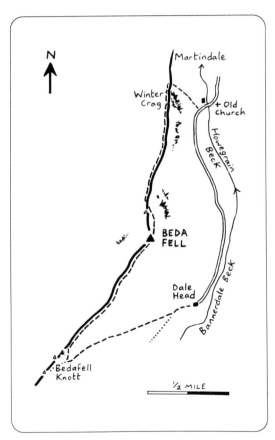

LOG OF THE WALKS

WALK	DATE	TIME Start	TIME Finish	WEATHER	COMMENTS
1					
2					
3					
4					
5					
6					
7					
8					
9					
10					
11					
12					
13					
14					

| 15 |
| 16 |
| 17 |
| 18 |
| 19 |
| 20 |
| 21 |
| 22 |
| 23 |
| 24 |
| 25 |
| 26 |
| 27 |
| 28 |
| 29 |
| 30 |

HILLSIDE GUIDES

  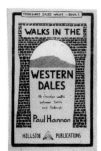

LONG DISTANCE WALKS - LAKE DISTRICT

LONG DISTANCE WALKS - NORTHERN ENGLAND

CIRCULAR WALKS - YORKSHIRE DALES